A
GARDENER'S BOUQUET
OF
QUOTATIONS

A GARDENER'S BOUQUET OF

QUOTATIONS

COMPILED AND EDITED BY

Maria Polushkin Robbins

THE ECCO PRESS

THE ECCO PRESS
100 West Broad Street
Hopewell, New Jersey 08525

Published simultaneously in Canada by
Penguin Books Canada Ltd., Ontario
Printed in the United States of America

Library of Congress Cataloging-in-Publication Data

A Gardener's bouquet of quotations / compiled and edited by Maria
Polushkin Robbins. — 1st Ecco ed.
p. cm
Includes index
ISBN 0-88001-589-6
1. Gardens—Quotations, maxims, etc.   2. Gardening—Quotations,
maxims, etc.   I. Polushkin, Maria.
PN6084.G33G37   1998
808.8'2—dc21   97-33092

Designed by Eve L. Kirch
The text of this book is set in Goudy Old Style

9 8 7 6 5 4 3 2 1

FIRST ECCO EDITION 1998

This book is for Sally,
who loves to read and to garden,
and is still blooming
in her ninety-second year.

ACKNOWLEDGMENTS

For ideas, inspiration, sources, citations, book loans and much needed moral support, I want to thank my sister, Lydia; Pat Strachan; Winnie Rosen; Joanna Grossman; Genie Chipps; Robyn Low; Tom Parrish; my friend and beloved agent, Faith Hornby Hamlin; and my husband, Ken, who managed to be incredibly helpful on this book without knowing anything at all (as nearly as I can tell) about gardening.

Index cards have always been a mainstay for anyone collecting quotations, but I have come to know that for this purpose computers are better. Special thanks to Zig Schmitt, Gary Rieveschl and Stephen Taylor, my personal, unofficial, but always on line tech support team.

CONTENTS

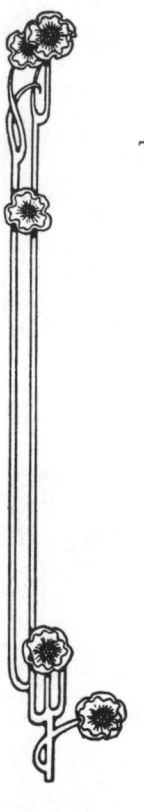
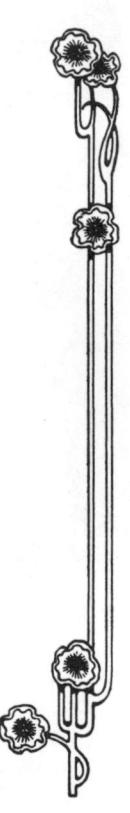

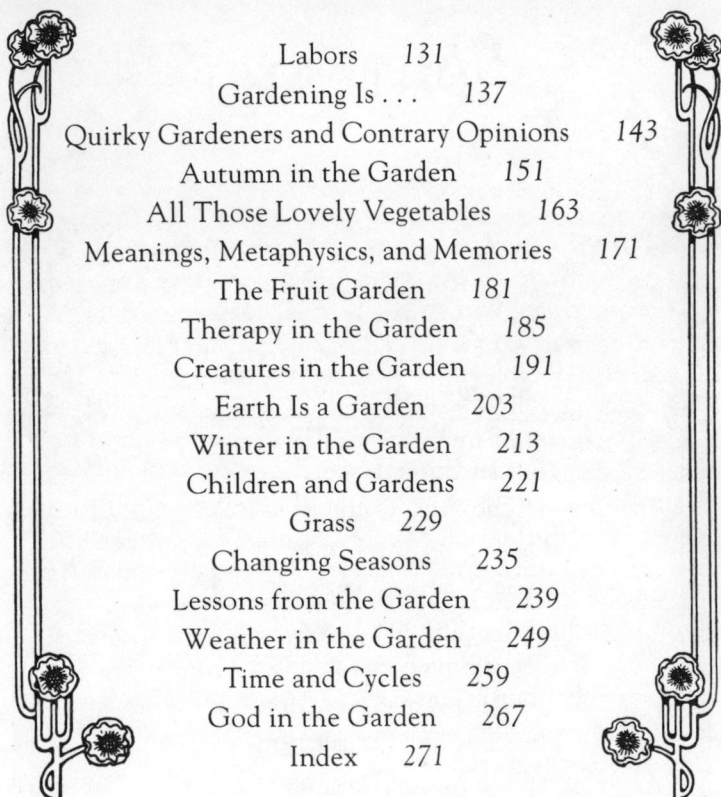

PREFACE

There are, of course, as many kinds of gardeners in the world as there are gardens, and I have come to know my place among them: I am at heart, I now realize, an armchair gardener, though I do still poke around in various unkempt flower and vegetable beds. Over the years I have begun hundreds of grandiose garden projects, all of which, in all their messy stages of incompletion, haunt me. My real garden, however, consists of many large, untidy piles of books and magazines, and files upon files of clippings. Other gardeners dream during idle winter months of warm weather when they can once again feel the springy earth responding to the labor of their hands and backs; I resent having to abandon the lazy, languid hours spent reading about other people's gardens, their problems, their solutions, their labors, heartaches and triumphs. Confronting the hard realities of my own garden seems so uncozy.

The flimsiest excuse, the slightest failure, will often suffice to send me back indoors for the consolation of plowing through words instead of earth, culling the fruit of other's struggles, stealing flowers from other's gardens, collecting them into bouquets of words, thoughts, advice and warning, inspiration and imagination.

This book, as you now see, is my excuse and atonement for having spent so many guilty hours in such comfortable pleasures. I hope it affords every gardener, every would-be gardener, even every might-have-been gardener a good excuse to sink into a choice armchair and live vicariously for a while, enjoying the pleasures of a hundred different gardens, and suffering the very bearable sorrows of garden tragedies that are easily soothed by a hot cup of tea—bolstered all the while by the smug certainty that you, of course, will do much, much better.

In most climates gardeners spend nearly half the year indoors dreaming and scheming, and making the whole affair at least as cogitative as it is sensual. That's probably why gardeners are such inveterate readers. And it is well to remember that in the garden, Nature and human artifice are as nearly allied in purpose as those two ancient enemies are ever likely to be. Which in turn, perhaps, is why writing and gardening seem to enjoy a natural affinity.

In any case, the garden writing sampled herein seems to divide itself naturally into a few broad types: There are, first of all, gardeners who write in order to share with others what they have learned and experienced in the garden. This is typical of the generosity of gardeners in general, although Henry Mitchell, a most generous writer, contributes this caveat:

Those new to gardening should know, however, that most gardeners hate to part with dirt, clay pots, pickle jars, really good labels, stakes, tarred twine, and any kind of wooden box. They do not mind giving a plant that sells for $40 if they have an extra one, but the other stuff (which may be worth a dime) it tears the heart to part with.

Then there are writers who garden, and so naturally enough consider gardening a worthy subject for their pens—Vita Sackville-West, May Sarton, and Thoreau come immediately to mind. These writers are apt to wax rhapsodic about the esthetic or even moral virtues of the garden, and are inclined to vivid description and even metaphor. Here Colette waxes not merely rhapsodic, but positively Freudian:

How can one help shivering with delight when one's hot fingers close around the stem of a live flower, cool from the shade and stiff with newborn vigor.

There are also writers who, though not particularly interested in gardening themselves, are nevertheless astute observers and interested in the natural world around them—Willa Cather, E. F. Benson, Doris Lessing, and John Steinbeck are just a few examples. Here is Robert Frost:

Nature does not complete things. She is chaotic. Man must finish, and he does so by making a garden and building a wall.

Finally, while most of the writers quoted in this anthology express an affection for their subject in one way or another, there are those to whom gardening is a pointless activity and a waste of time. Ralph Waldo Emerson says as much, although, I think, he equivocates just a bit:

> A garden is like those pernicious machineries which catch a man's coat-skirt or his hand, and draw in his arm, his leg, and his whole body to irresistible destruction.

Fran Lebowitz, on the other hand, is more or less unequivocal:

> I am not the type who wants to go back to the land; I am the type who wants to go back to the hotel.

I knew I liked them.

By planting flowers one invites butterflies . . . by planting pines one invites the wind . . . by planting bananas one invites the rain, and by planting willow trees one invites the cicadas.

— CHAO CH'ANG

✿ ✿ ✿

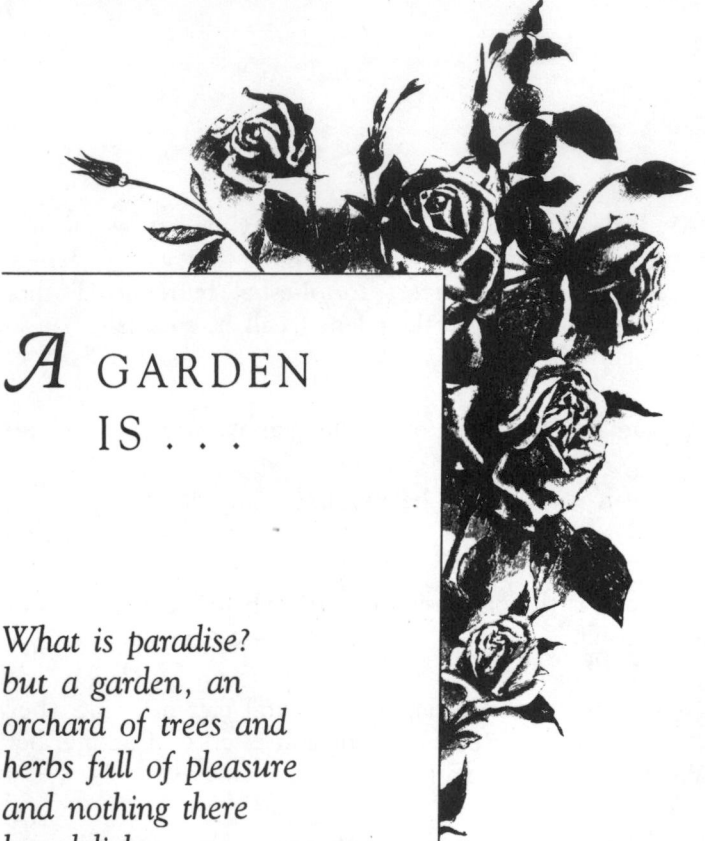

A GARDEN IS . . .

What is paradise?
but a garden, an
orchard of trees and
herbs full of pleasure
and nothing there
but delights.

—WILLIAM LAWSON

"My little plot," said Miss Mapp. "Very modest, as you see, three quarters of an acre at the most, but well screened. My flower beds: sweet roses, tortoiseshell butterflies. Rather a nice clematis. My little Eden, I call it, so small, but so well beloved."　　　　　　　　　　　　—E. F. BENSON

All gardens are a form of autobiography.　—ROBERT DASH

A garden is a thing of beauty and a job forever.
　　　　　　　　　　　　　　　　　　—ANONYMOUS

A garden is the one spot on earth where history does not assert itself.　　　　　　　　　　—SIR EDMUND GOSSE

As gardens are to the Japanese a vital part of living, they must not only express the spirit and essence of nature, but also the dignity of man.　　　　　　　—SAMUEL NEWSOM

But gardens are places in which men come home again, in which they realize, that "Art itself is nature."
　　　　　　　　　　　　　　　　　—TERRY COMITO

Every garden is a chore sometimes, but no real garden is nothing but a chore. —NANCY GRASBY

Gardens are the result of a collaboration between art and nature. —PENELOPE HOBHOUSE

Gardens, scholars say, are the first sign of commitment to a community. When people plant corn they are saying, let's stay here. And by their connection to the land, they are connected to one another. —ANNE RAVER

If you really want to draw close to your garden, you must remember first of all that you are dealing with a being that lives and dies; like the human body, with its poor flesh, its illnesses at times repugnant. One must not always see it dressed up for a ball, manicured and immaculate. —FERNAND LEQUENNE

Until now the garden has been like some dainty hesitant maid, coyly proffering an occasional delicate gift with one shy timorous hand while mysteriously withholding the other behind her back. Her limbs are as yet a bit angular, but promising in their sweetly generous proportions a rounded fulfillment for the future. Her face is mistily veiled, the petal-like lids of her azure eyes hardly lifted to reveal the abundant promise of riches beneath her gentle breasts. Her lips are rosily parted in the eager delight of one who is about to confer beneficent gifts, and her breath is fragrant with the musk of warm air on parched earth and fresh-turned sod, the bouquet of unfolding frond and throbbing sap.

But now, as the hot sun of early summer pours his fecund rays upon her receptive form, she becomes the pregnant woman unfolding from dawn to dawn the gracious promise of fruition. Her limbs fill into rounded and ample curves; her breasts swell with nourishment; her eyes glow with secret knowledge, and her lips are curved with the fulfillment of life. —DELLA T. LUTES

No two gardens are the same. No two days are the same in one garden. —HUGH JOHNSON

Nothing is more completely the child of art than a garden. —SIR WALTER SCOTT

The cottage garden; most for use designed,
Yet not of beauty destitute. —CHARLOTTE SMITH

Oh! the things which happened in that garden! If you have never had a garden you cannot understand, and if you had a garden you will know that it would take a whole book to describe all that came to pass there. At first it seemed that green things would never cease pushing their way through the earth, in the grass, in the beds, even in the crevices of the walls. Then the green things began to show buds and the buds began to unfurl and show color, every shade of blue, every shade of purple, every tint and hue of

crimson. . . . Iris and white lilies rose out of the grass in
sheaves, and the green alcoves filled themselves with amaz-
ing armies of the blue and white flower lances of tall delphiniums or columbines or campanulas.

—FRANCES HODGSON BURNETT

You can't forget a garden
When you have planted seed—
When you have watched the weather
And know a rose's need.

—LOUISE DRISCOLL

*You don't have a garden just for
yourself. You have it to share.*

—AUGUSTA CARTER

ઠ૭

Sweet is the rose, but grows upon a brere;
Sweet is the Junipere, but sharp his bough;
Sweet is the Eglantine, but pricketh nere;
Sweet is the Firbloom, but his branches rough;
Sweet is the Cypresse, but his rynd is tough;
Sweet is the nut, but bitter is his pill;
Sweet is the Broome-flowre, but yet sowre enough;
And sweet is Moly, but his root is ill.

So every sweet with soure is tempered still,
That maketh it be coveted the more:
For easie things, that may be got at will,
Most sorts of men doe set but little store.
—EDMUND SPENSER

I could live in Paris only if I had a beautiful garden.
—COLETTE

A city garden, especially of one who has no other, ought to be planted and ornamented with all possible care.
—MARCUS PORCIUS CATO

Like people everywhere, and perhaps more than most, city dwellers want and need gardens and growing things.
—LYNDEN B. MILLER

A house without a garden is a house with no foundation at all, a house subject to all the hazards of life. But a garden with no house is a garden with no soul.
—FERNAND LEQUENNE

As every estate agent knows, a poor house in good sur-roundings will sell for a higher price than a better house in poor surroundings, and in a town they confidently ask 25 percent more rent for a flat with a view of a park than for an identical flat with no view.
—NAN FAIRBROTHER

I am quite of the opinion that a garden should look as though it belonged to a house, and the house as though it were conscious of and approved the garden. In passing from one to the other, one should experience no sense of discord, but the sensations produced by the one should be continued, with a delicate difference, by the other. —ALFRED AUSTIN

It may be argued further that real beauty is neither in garden nor landscape, but in the relation of both to the individual, that what we are seeing is not only a scenic setting for pool and fountain and parterre, but a background for life. —SIR GEORGE SITWELL

Someone has described personal charm as an open secret, that is precisely the character of an old garden.

—FRANCIS INIGO THOMAS

A plant is like a self-willed man, out of whom we can obtain all which we desire, if we will only treat him his own way.   —JOHANN WOLFGANG VON GOETHE

A little garden square and wall'd;
And in it throve an ancient evergreen,
A yew-tree, and all round it ran a walk
Of shingle, and a walk divided it.

—ALFRED, LORD TENNYSON

The tiniest garden is often the loveliest.

—VITA SACKVILLE-WEST

Americans must be far more brotherly-hearted than we are, for they do not seem to mind being over-looked. They have no sense of private enclosure. They never plant hedges to cut themselves off from the gaze of the passerby, nor do they plant hedges between their own garden and their neighbor's. All is open. Walk in, walk in! they seem to say, in cordial invitation.   —VITA SACKVILLE-WEST

He hath a garden circummured with brick,
Whose western side is with a vineyard back'd;
And to that vineyard is a planched gate,
That makes his opening with this bigger key:
This other doth command a little door,
Which from the vineyard to the garden leads.

—WILLIAM SHAKESPEARE

He missed, it is true, the hawthorn hedges of England; those beautiful walls of verdure whose only fault is that their impervious foliage shuts out from view the fields they inclose; while the open fences of America allow the stranger to regale his eye, and satisfy his curiosity with a free prospect of the country through which he is travelling.

—ELIZA LESLIE

I saugh a Gardin right anoon
Ful long and brood and everydel
Enclos it was and walled wel
With hye walles embatailled.

—CHAUCER

It was the sweetest, most mysterious-looking place anyone could imagine. The high walls which shut it in were covered with leafless stems of climbing roses which were so thick that they were matted together. . . . All the ground was covered with grass of a wintry brown and out of it grew clumps of bushes which were surely rosebushes if they were alive. There were numbers of standard roses which had so spread their branches that they were like little trees. There were other trees in the garden, and one of the things which made the place look strangest and loveliest was that climbing roses had run all over them and swung down long tendrils which made light swaying curtains, and here and there they had caught at each other or at a far-reaching branch and had crept from one tree to another and made lovely bridges of themselves.

—FRANCES HODGSON BURNETT

My Garden sweet, enclosed with walles strong,
Enbanked with benches to sytt and take my rest:
The Knotts so enknotted, it cannot be exprest,
With arbors and alyes so pleasaunt and so dulce.

—GEORGE CAVENDISH

One family builds a wall and two families get the benefit of it.   —CHINESE PROVERB

Over the garden wall,
The sweetest girl of all;
There never were yet
Such eyes of jet,
And you may bet
I'll never forget
The night our lips in kisses met
Over the garden wall.

—HARRY HUNTER

The great challenge for the garden designer is not to make the garden look natural, but to make the garden so that the people in it will feel natural.   —LAWRENCE HALPRIN

Try to keep a garden beautiful to yourself alone and see what happens—the neighbor, hurrying by to catch his train of mornings, will stop to snatch a glint of joy from the iris purpling by your doorstep. The motorist will throw on brakes and back downhill just to see those Oriental poppies massed against the wall.   —RICHARDSON WRIGHT

Walls are so necessary for Gardens, that even to multiply them, I make as many little gardens as I can in the Neighborhood of the Great one, whereby I have not only Wallfruits or Espaliers and shelter, which is very considerable; but am also thereby enabled to correct some defects and irregularities which would render the Garden disagreeable.
   —DE LA QUINTINYE

You'll never have a garden—a garden needs walls and you have no walls.   —RUSSELL PAGE

And nearer to the river's trembling edge
There grew broad flag-flowers, purple, pranked with white,
And starry river buds among the sedge,
And floating water-lilies, broad and bright.
   —PERCY BYSSHE SHELLEY

Give space to reflecting water. Even if it means giving up flowers (which of course it necessarily does). Less color and more lily pool are better than more color and less lily pool.
—HENRY MITCHELL

Pleasure gardens are outdoor places designed by man which induce in the beholder a sense of well-being. Like drugs, they can be addictive, but unlike drugs, they have no unpleasant after-effects unless the addict undertakes to create a pleasure garden of his own, when he must resign himself to unremitting backaching toil, first in creating the garden and then in preventing nature from reclaiming her territory.
—RONALD KING

Everywhere water is a thing of beauty gleaming in the dewdrop, singing in the summer rain.
—JOHN BALLANTINE GOUGH

THE PESKY PROBLEM
OF WEEDS

Sweet flowers are slow and weeds make haste.

—WILLIAM SHAKESPEARE

A good garden may have some weeds.   —PROVERB

A weed is no more than a flower in disguise,
Which is seen through at once, if love give a man eyes.
                              —JAMES RUSSELL LOWELL

Advice on dandelions:
If you can't beat them, eat them.
                              —DR. JAMES DUKE, BOTANIST

And so it criticized each flower
This supercilious seed;
Until it woke one summer hour,
And found itself a weed.
                              —MILDRED HOWELLS

But a weed is simply a plant that wants to grow where
people want something else. In blaming nature, people mistake the culprit. Weeds are people's idea, not nature's.
                              —ANONYMOUS

Lilies that fester smell far worse than weeds.
                                    —WILLIAM SHAKESPEARE

Love of flowers and vegetables is not enough to make a good gardener. He must also hate weeds.
                                    —EUGENE P. BERTIN

Many things grow in the garden that were never sowed there.   —THOMAS FULLER

Now 'tis spring, and weeds are shallow rooted;
Suffer them now and they'll o'ergrow the garden.
                                    —WILLIAM SHAKESPEARE

Originally, the word "weeds" was we'ods, and it was the Anglo-Saxon name for all herbs and small plants. . . . To past generations of men, all plants were regarded with respect.   —AUDREY WYNNE-HATFIELD

Our attitude towards plants is a singularly narrow one. If we see any immediate utility in a plant we foster it. If for any reason we find its presence undesirable or merely a matter of indifference, we may condemn it to destruction forthwith.   —RACHEL CARSON

To gardeners, onion grass is a harbinger not of spring's delights but of chickweed, bindweed, knotweed, pigweed plantain, purslane and all the other intruders that will spoil their little Edens—nature's backhanded way, gardeners feel, of making them pay for some original horticultural sin.

—ANONYMOUS

The frost hurts not weeds. —THOMAS FULLER

Too many people make their leisure activities work. In gardening, you can become a slave to your circumstances, spending the entire weekend weeding. —ELLEN GOODMAN

You fight dandelions all weekend, and late Monday afternoon there they are, pert as all get out, in full and gorgeous bloom, pretty as can be, thriving as only dandelions can in the face of adversity.

—HAL BORLAND

Weeds never die.   —DANISH PROVERB

What would become of the garden if the gardener treated
all the weeds and slugs and birds and trespassers as he would
like to be treated, if he were in their place?
                                    —THOMAS HENRY HUXLEY

When I have trouble writing, I step outside my studio into
the garden and pull weeds until my mind clears—I find
weeding to be the best therapy there is for writer's block.
                                         —IRVING STONE

He who wants to eat a good supper should eat a weed of every kind.   —ITALIAN PROVERB

No garden without its weeds.   —THOMAS FULLER

Spring in the Garden

I have seen the lady April bringing
the daffodils,
Bringing the springing grass and the
soft warm April rain.

—John Masefield

I love spring anywhere, but if I could choose I would always greet it in a garden. —RUTH STOUT

First a howling blizzard woke us,
Then the rain came down to soak us,
And now before the eye can focus—
Crocus.
　　　　　　　　　　—LILJA ROGERS

I have said that there was great pleasure in watching the ways in which different plants come through the ground, and February and March are the months in which that can best be seen. —HENRY N. ELLACOMBE

A light exists in Spring
Not present in the year
at any other period
When March is scarcely here.
　　　　　　　　—EMILY DICKINSON

Where did Gabriel get a lily,
In the month of March,
When the green
Is hardly seen
On the early larch?
—GRACE JAMES

March is a month of considerable frustration—it is so near
spring and yet across a great deal of the country the weather
is still so violent and changeable that outdoor activity in
our yards seems light-years away.   —THALASSA CRUSO

April comes like an idiot,
babbling and strewing flowers.
—EDNA ST. VINCENT MILLAY

April's rare capricious loveliness.   —JULIA DORR

A violet in the youth of primy nature,
Forward, not permanent, sweet, not lasting,
The perfume and suppliance of a minute.
—WILLIAM SHAKESPEARE

I had not thought of violets of late,
The wild, shy kind that springs beneath your feet
In wistful April days.   —ALICE DUNBAR-NELSON

Surely as cometh the Winter, I know
There are Spring violets under the snow.
                              —R. H. NEWELL

The blue eyes of Springtime.   —HEINRICH HEINE

April, April,
Laugh thy girlish laughter;
Then, the moment after,
Weep thy girlish tears.
        —SIR WILLIAM WATSON

Spongy April.   —WILLIAM SHAKESPEARE

Well-apparel'd April on the heel
Of limping Winter treads.
        —WILLIAM SHAKESPEARE

Almost any farmer can describe blackberry winter.
    It's that cold spell that comes in May, about three weeks
after spring fever. It comes when blackberries are in bloom
and does sometimes actually drop a few real snowflakes into
the white flowers. It doesn't bite through to the hard, green,
incipient berries nestled behind the petals. It lasts less than
a week.   —RACHEL PEDEN

Blackberry winter, the time when hoarfrost lies on the blackberry blossoms; without this frost the berries will not set. It is the forerunner of a rich harvest.

—MARGARET MEAD

Daffodils,
That come before the swallow dares, and take
The winds of March with beauty.

—WILLIAM SHAKESPEARE

*I wandered lonely as a cloud
That floats on high o'er vales and hills,
When all at once I saw a crowd,
A host, of golden daffodils.*

—WILLIAM WORDSWORTH

❧ ❧ ❧

When we were in the woods beyond Gowbarrow park we saw a few daffodils close to the waterside. . . . But as we went along there were more and yet more and at last under the boughs of the trees, we saw that there was a long belt of them along the shore, about the breadth of a country turnpike road. I never saw daffodils so beautiful they grew about the mossy stones about and about them, some rested their heads upon these stones as on a pillow for weariness and the rest tossed and reeled and danced and seemed as if they verily laughed with the wind that blew upon them over the lake.

—DOROTHY WORDSWORTH

Forsythia is pure joy. There is not an ounce, not a glimmer of sadness or even *knowledge* in forsythia. Pure, undiluted, untouched joy. —ANNE MORROW LINDBERGH

> Fast fading violets cover'd up in leaves;
> And mid-May's eldest child,
> The coming musk-rose, full of dewy wine,
> The murmurous haunt of flies on summer eves.
>
> —JOHN KEATS

Flowers before May bring bad luck. —WELSH PROVERB

Horticulturally, the month of May is opening night, Home-coming, and Graduation Day all rolled into one.

—TAM MOSSMAN

Rough winds do shake the darling buds of May.

—WILLIAM SHAKESPEARE

You are as welcome as the flowers in May.

—CHARLES MACKLIN

It is dry, hazy June weather. We are more of the earth, farther from heaven these days.

—HENRY DAVID THOREAU

It is the month of June,
The month of leaves and roses
When pleasant sights salute the eyes,
And pleasant scents the noses.

—N. P. WILLIS

June brings tulips, lilies, roses,
Fills the children's hands with posies. —SARA COLERIDGE

On this June day the buds in my garden are almost as enchanting as the open flowers. Things in bud bring, in the heat of a June noontide, the recollection of the loveliest days of the year—those days in May when all is suggested, nothing yet fulfilled. —MRS. FRANCIS KING

Lilacs, False blue, White, Purple,
Colour of lilac,
Your great puffs of flowers
Are everywhere in this my New England. . . .
Lilacs in dooryards
Holding quiet conversation with an early moon;
Lilacs watching a deserted house; . . .
Lilacs, wind-beaten, staggering under a lopsided shock of bloom,
You are everywhere.

—AMY LOWELL

Again rejoicing Nature sees
Her robe assume its vernal hues
Her leafy locks wave in the breeze,
All freshly steep'd in morning dews.
—ROBERT BURNS

And then the rain began, the tonic, greening, transforming rain that comes only once a year.

At gray daylight, silver drops still clung to the undersides of peach limbs; but the rain had stopped, and now every living blade and stalk whose destiny it is to be green was suddenly astonishingly green.
—RACHEL PEDEN

Anyone who has a bulb has spring.
Bulbs don't need much light; they don't need good soil;
and they don't need cosseting. They are, in fact, the horticultural equivalent of cats: self-contained, easy-care and su-
premely suited to living in New York.   —ANONYMOUS

Autumn arrives in the early morning, but spring at the
close of a winter day.   —ELIZABETH BOWEN

Come, gentle Spring! Ethereal Mildness! Come.
—JAMES THOMSON

*B*uttercups and daisies,
    Oh, the pretty flowers;
Coming ere the spring time,
    To tell of sunny hours.
When the trees are leafless;
    When the fields are bare;
Buttercups and daisies
    Spring up here and there.
        —MARY HOWITT

❧ ❧ ❧

Hoe while it is spring, and enjoy the best anticipations. It is not much matter if things do not turn out well.

—CHARLES DUDLEY WARNER

I have walked this south stream when to believe in spring was an act of faith. It was spitting snow and blowing, and within two days of being May. . . . But as if to assert the triumph of climate over weather, one ancient willow managed a few gray pussy willows, soft and barely visible against the snow-blurred gray background.   —ANN ZWINGER

If in my gardens only, nowhere else,
The flowers of spring should bloom,
Even the man who has neglected me
To gaze on them would surely come.
                        —IZUMI SHIKIBU

In the spring, at the end of the day, you should smell like dirt.   —MARGARET ATWOOD

It always seems to me that the herbaceous peony is the very epitome of June. Larger than any rose, it has something of the cabbage rose's voluminous quality; and when it finally drops from the vase, it sheds its vast petticoats with a bump on the table, all in an intact heap, much as a rose will suddenly fall, making us look up from our book or conversation, to notice for one moment the death of what had still appeared to be a living beauty.   —VITA SACKVILLE-WEST

It is in this unearthly first hour of spring twilight that earth's almost agonized livingness is most felt. This hour is so dreadful to some people that they hurry indoors and turn on the lights. —ELIZABETH BOWEN

Just now the lilac is in bloom,
All before my little room.
—RUPERT BROOKE

Now every field is clothed with grass, and every tree with leaves; now the woods put forth their blossoms, and the year assumes its gay attire. —VIRGIL

Now Nature hangs her mantle green
On every blooming tree,
And spreads her sheets o' daisies white
Out o'er the grassy lea.
—ROBERT BURNS

Spring comes: the flowers learn their colored shapes.
—MARIA KONOPNICKA

Spring has come when you can put your foot on three daisies at once. —ANONYMOUS

Spring is sooner recognized by plants than by men.
—CHINESE PROVERB

Spring would not be spring without bird songs.

—FRANCIS M. CHAPMAN

The air and the earth interpenetrated in the warm gusts of spring; the soil was full of sunlight, and the sunlight full of red dust. The air one breathed was saturated with earthy smells, and the grass under foot had a reflection of the blue sky in it.   —WILLA CATHER

The country habit has me by the heart,
For he's bewitched forever who has seen,
Not with his eyes but with his vision, Spring
Flow down the woods and stipple leaves with sun.
                              —VITA SACKVILLE-WEST

The fields breathe sweet, the daisies kiss our feet,
Young lovers meet, old wives a-sunning sit,
In every street these tunes our ears do greet,
    Cuckoo, jug-jug, pu-we, to-witta-woo!
        Spring! the sweet Spring!
                              —THOMAS NASHE

The first day of spring was once the time for taking the young virgins into the fields, there in dalliance to set an example in fertility for Nature to follow. Now we just set the clock an hour ahead and change the oil in the crankcase.   —E. B. WHITE

The flowers appear on the earth; the time of the singing of birds is come, and the voice of the turtle is heard in our land.   —THE SONG OF SOLOMON

The last fling of winter is over. . . . The earth, the soil itself, has a dreaming quality about it. It is warm now to the touch; it has come alive; it hides secrets that in a moment, in a little while, it will tell.
                    —DONALD CULROSS PEATTIE

The naked earth is warm with Spring,
And with green grass and bursting trees
Leans to the sun's kiss glorying,
And quivers in the sunny breeze.
—JULIAN GRENFELL

The snow has left the cottage top;
    The thatch-moss grows in brighter green;
And eaves in quick succession drop,
    Where grinning icicles have been,
Pit-patting with a pleasant noise
    In tubs set by the cottage-door;
While duck and geese, with happy joys,
    Plunge in the yard-pond brimming o'er.
The sun peeps through the window pane;
    Which children mark with laughing eye,
And in the wet street steal again
    To tell each other spring is nigh.
—JOHN CLARE

The year's at the Spring
And day's at the morn;
Morning's at seven;
The hillside's dew-pearled;
The lark's on the wing;
The snail's on the thorn:
God's in his Heaven—
All's right with the world!
—ROBERT BROWNING

The mysterious force of spring rules.   —ALEXANDER FET

> When daffodils begin to peer,
> With the heigh! the doxy over the dale,
> Why, then comes in the sweet o' the year;
> For the red blood reigns in the winter's pale.
>   —WILLIAM SHAKESPEARE

When there's new growth bursting out all over, everything fresh, green, and flourishing, the plants are little rockets of success going off every time you look at them.
                              —JACQUELINE HERITEAU

> Ye may trace my step o'er the wakening earth,
> By the winds which tell of the violet's birth,
> By the primrose-stars in the shadowy grass,
> By the green leaves opening as I pass.
>   —FELICIA HEMANS

THE FLOWER GARDEN

Space for the sunflower,
Bright with yellow glow
To court the sky.

—CAROLINE GILMAN

When we learn to call flowers by name we take the first step toward a real intimacy with them.

—Mrs. William Starr Dana

As for marigolds, poppies, hollyhocks, and valorous sunflowers, we shall never have a garden without them, both for their own sake, and for the sake of old-fashioned folks, who used to love them. —Henry Ward Beecher

Flowers of all heavens, and lovelier than their names.

—Alfred, Lord Tennyson

Flowers changed the face of the planet. Without them, the world we know—even man himself—would never have existed. —Loren Eiseley

All those faces! Most of them smiling, some of them scowling . . . some like little children, lit with a radiant innocence, others like small floral villains, their petals freaked with dark and dangerous hues. No two faces are the same, and as you stare and stare at this multicoloured host, you

find yourself making up stories about them, you send them marching on great adventures, and even if the thunder growls, it seems to come from over the hills and far away.
—BEVERLEY NICHOLS

How splendid in the morning glows the lily; with what grace he throws
His supplication to the rose.   —JAMES ELROY FLECKER

Oh, this is the joy of the rose:
That it blows,
And goes.
—WILLA CATHER

One could not pluck a flower without troubling a star.
—FRANCIS THOMPSON

One of the attractive things about flowers is their beautiful reserve.   —HENRY DAVID THOREAU

People from a planet without flowers would think we must be mad with joy the whole time to have such things about us.   —IRIS MURDOCH

See how the flowers, as at parade,
Under their colours stand display'd:
Each regiment in order grows,
That of the tulip, pink, and rose.
—ANDREW MARVELL

The Amen! of Nature is always a flower.
—OLIVER WENDELL HOLMES

The Sun-flower: ... this bright and constant flower ena-
moured of the sun.   —MARGUERITE BLESSINGTON

*Within the garden's peaceful scene
Appear'd two lovely foes,
Aspiring to the rank of queen,
The Lily and the Rose.*
—WILLIAM COWPER

I have come to understand the unspeakable loveliness of a solitary spray of blossoms arranged as only a Japanese expert knows how to arrange it—not simply poking the spray into a vase, but by perhaps one whole hour's labor of trimming and posing and daintiest manipulation—and therefore I cannot think now of what we Occidentals call a "bouquet" as anything but a vulgar murdering of flowers, an outrage upon the color sense, a brutality, an abomination.

—LAFCADIO HEARN

The white chrysanthemum
Even when lifted to the eye
Remains immaculate.

—BASHO

Chrysanthemums, which in their art shades of mauve, and terra-cotta and russet, smell of moths, camphorball, and drowned sailors.   —SIR OSBERT SITWELL

Daylilies are dangerous, however, and absolutely addicting, except for the occasional gardener with a will of steel and a heart of carborundum. Someone gave me one once and I was trapped. It's been my experience that most of the friends to whom I give a few come sidling up the next year to ask for more, perhaps even to get the address of the American Hemerocallis Society so they can sign up. If they do, they're probably doomed for life. The addiction may go into remission, but it never goes away.   —ALLEN LACY

Everything is handsome about the geranium not excepting its name. —LEIGH HUNT

I will have no more tall bearded irises. The love affair has ended. —ALLEN LACY

Remember that the most beautiful things in the world are the most useless; peacocks and lilies for instance.
—JOHN RUSKIN

The Lily:
The careless eye can find no grace,
No beauty in the scaly folds,
Nor see within the dark embrace
What latent loveliness it hold.
Yet in that bulb, those sapless scales,
The lily wraps her silver vest.
—MARY TIGHE

We once had a lily here that bore 108 flowers on one stalk: it was photographed, naturally, for all the gardening papers. The bees came from miles and miles, and there were the most disgraceful Bacchanalian scenes: bees hardly able to find their way home. —EDITH SITWELL

The fattest and most scrumptious of all flowers, a rare fusion of fluff and majesty, the peony is now coming into bloom.

—HENRY MITCHELL

I think for wonderous variety, for certain picturesque qualities, for color and form and a subtle mystery of character,
Poppies seem, on the whole, the most satisfactory flowers
among the annuals.   —CELIA THAXTER

There is something very fine about a poppy, in the extraordinary combination of boldness of color and great size with
its slender delicacy of stem, the grace of the set of the
beautiful buds, the fine turn of the flower as it opens, and
the wonderful airiness of poise of so heavy a flower. The
silkiness of tissue of the petals, and their semi-transparency
in some colors, and the delicate fringes of some varieties,
are great charms. . . . And when the flowers have shed, oh,
so lightly! their silken petals, there is still another beauty,
a seed vessel of such classic shape that it wears a crown.

—ELIZABETH LAWRENCE

All the year round she kept racks full of plants in pots standing on green-painted wooden steps. There were rare geraniums, dwarf rose bushes, spiraeas with misty white and pink plumes, a few "succulents," hairy and squat as crabs, and murderous cacti. —COLETTE

Tract upon tract of arrow bamboo danced in the wind like a solid ocean reaching far to the horizon, and on this ocean red clouds drifted. No! They were alpine rhododendrons bursting with joy. —TANG XIYANG

I'll say she looks as clear
As morning roses newly wash'd with dew.
—WILLIAM SHAKESPEARE

"I haven't much time to be fond of anything," says Sergeant Cuff. "But when I *have* a moment's fondness to bestow, most times . . . the roses get it." —WILKIE COLLINS

Gardeners don't really have to grow roses if they, like Bartleby the Scrivener, prefer not.   —ALLEN LACY

This morning we pulled ourselves together and went to a little village about thirty minutes away by bus, l'Hay des Roses, and walked through an immense rose garden just coming into bloom. Oh, at least a million roses, far too many, really. I should prefer about half an acre, with a dozen varieties very carefully chosen and tended. Some of those heavy dark red roses we used to have, some fine shell-pink-beige tea roses, Gold of Ophir, Gloire de Dijon, several climbing kinds, and a hedge or two of wild roses, and the whole thing surrounded by a carefully clipped wall of cape jessamines. I can see it, I know just how it should look. Some day I may even have it.

—KATHERINE ANNE PORTER

I don't know whether nice people tend to grow roses or growing roses makes people nice.   —ROLAND A. BROWNE

Jasmine is all in white and has many loves,
And the broom's betrothed to the bee;
But I will plight with the dainty rose,
For fairest of all is she.

—THOMAS HOOD

*My roses are my jewels, the sun
and moon my clocks, fruit and
water my food and drink.*

—HESTER LUCY STANHOPE

A Rose is sweeter in the bud than full blown.

—JOHN LYLY

Perhaps few people have ever asked themselves why they
admire a rose so much more than all other flowers. If they
consider, they will find, first, that red is, in a delicately
graduated state, the loveliest of all pure colors; and sec-
ondly, that in the rose there is no shadow, except which
is composed of color. All its shadows are fuller in color
than its lights, owing to the translucency and reflective
power of its leaves.   —JOHN RUSKIN

Preparing a bed for roses is a little like getting the house
ready for the arrival of a difficult old lady, some biddy with
aristocratic pretensions and persnickety tastes. Her stay is
bound to be an ordeal, and you want to give her as little
cause for complaint as possible.   —MICHAEL POLLAN

Red Rose, proud rose, sad rose of all my days!
Come near me while I sing the ancient ways.
                           —W. B. YEATS

Red roses unfurl.
In their calices burns the pearl.
             —SISTER BERTKEN

Rose is a rose is a rose is a rose.   —GERTRUDE STEIN

The cowslip is a country wench,
   The violet is a nun;—
But I will woo the dainty rose,
   The queen of every one.
               —THOMAS HOOD

There is no gathering the rose without being pricked by
the thorns.   —BIDAPI

Won't you come into the garden? I would like my roses to
see you.   —RICHARD BRINSLEY SHERIDAN

Clean as a lady,
cool as glass,
fresh without fragrance
the tulip was.
        —HUMBERT WOLFE

Here tulips bloom as they are told.   —RUPERT BROOKE

Not one of Flora's brilliant race
A form more perfect can display;
Art could not feign more simple grace
Nor Nature take a line away.
        —JAMES MONTGOMERY

A violet by the mossy stone
Half hidden from the eye!
Fair as a star when only one
Is shining in the sky.
        —WILLIAM WORDSWORTH

All through history violets have held a special place for their scent, their use and romance. The Greeks picked them for garlands and chaplets; the Romans made violet wine and fried them with slices of orange and lemon; the romantic poet Fortunas, Bishop of Poitiers, sent gifts of violets to St. Radegunde as decoration for her church. Perhaps best of all, the beautiful empress Josephine embroidered her wedding dress with violets, after which they were a signature of love between her and Napoleon. No other flower so small has been held in such high esteem as Viola odorata.   —ROSEMARY VEREY

Do you think amethysts can be the souls of good violets?
                                    —L. M. MONTGOMERY

Sir,

   You asked me to come and spend a week with you, which means I would be near my daughter, whom I adore. You who live with her know how rarely I see her, how much her presence delights me, and I'm touched that you should ask me to come and see her. All the same I'm not going to accept your kind invitation, for the time being at any rate. The reason is that my pink cactus is probably going to flower. It's a very rare plant I've been given, and I'm told that in our climate it flowers only once every four years. Now, I am already a very old woman, and if I went away when my pink cactus is about to flower, I'm certain I shouldn't see it flower again.

So I beg you, sir, to accept my sincere thanks and my regrets, together with my kind regards.

—SIDONIE COLETTE (Colette's mother),
    to her son-in-law
    written when she was seventy-six;
    she died a year later.

GARDENERS DEFINED

Gardeners, I think, dream bigger dreams than emperors.

—MARY CANTWELL

My liking for gardens to be lavish is an inherent part of my garden philosophy. I like generosity wherever I find it, whether in gardens or elsewhere. I hate to see things scrimp and scrubby. Even the smallest garden can be prodigal within its limitations.　　　　　—VITA SACKVILLE-WEST

Show me your garden and I shall tell you what you are.
　　　　　　　　　　　　　　　　　—ALFRED AUSTIN

As is the garden such is the gardener.
A man's nature runs either to herbs or weeds.
　　　　　　　　　　　　　　　　　—FRANCIS BACON

The would-be gardener requires more patience than most mortals!　　　　　　　　　　　　—CELIA THAXTER

An old woman in blue jeans, lugging pails of sand or humus, handling fork or spade, may be an edifying sight, but it is hardly the picture of leisured dignity one would like to present.　　　　　　—BUNKER HOLLINGSWORTH

But in the garden, lying on your back, say, looking at the spined soldier bug devour a potato beetle and make love to his mate at the same time, you have returned to a certain level of life usually forgotten in the 9 to 5. Gardeners can spend hours like this, and it's hard to explain to nongardeners.... Maybe you have to be there.   —ANNE RAVER

Compared to gardeners, I think it is generally agreed that others understand very little about anything of consequence.   —HENRY MITCHELL

Did you ever hear of planting hands? ... Well, I can only tell you what it feels like. It's when you're picking off the buds you don't want. Everything goes right down into your fingertips. You watch your fingers work. They do it themselves. You can feel how it is. They pick and pick the buds. They never make a mistake. They're with the plant. Do you see? Your fingers and the plant. You can feel that, right up your arm. They know. They never make a mistake. You can feel it. When you're like that you can't do anything wrong. Do you see that? Can you understand that?
    —JOHN STEINBECK

Every novice gardener made the mistake of wanting rewards at once, and she smiled to recognize the failing in herself. But recognition didn't stop her from pursuing what she wanted.   —ROSIE THOMAS

For a high minded man agriculture is the best of all occupations. —XENOPHON

Gardens cannot be considered in detachment from the people who made them. —DEREK CLIFFORD

Have feminists ever fully assessed the role of women in horticulture? It is a prodigious one. —RONALD BLYTHE

I have never, for any eight months together, during my whole life, been without a garden. —WILLIAM COBBETT

If you bee not able, nor willing to hyre a gardner, keepe your profites to your self, but then you must take all the paines. —WILLIAM LAWSON

Men seem more obsessed with order in the garden than women. —MIRABEL OSLER

Of the seven deadly sins, surely it is pride that most commonly afflicts the gardener.

—MICHAEL POLLAN

❧ ❧ ❧

Oh, tell me how my garden grows,
Where I no more may take delight,
And if some dream of me it knows,
Who dream of it by day and night.
—MILDRED HOWELLS

Old gardeners never die, they just spade away.
—MURIEL COX

Only man deliberately rearranges the setting he lives in simply because he prefers the look of it.
—NAN FAIRBROTHER

The first three men in the world were a gardener, a ploughman, and a grazier.   —ABRAHAM COWLEY

The home gardener is part scientist, part artist, part philosopher, part plowman. He modifies the climate around his home.   —JOHN R. WHITING

The man who has planted a garden feels that he has done something for the good of the world.
—CHARLES DUDLEY WARNER

The most noteworthy thing about gardeners is that they are always optimistic, always enterprising, and never satisfied. They always look forward to doing better than they have ever done before.
—VITA SACKVILLE-WEST

There is no ancient gentlemen but gardeners. . . .
They hold up Adam's profession.
—WILLIAM SHAKESPEARE

There, with her baskets and spades and clippers, and wearing her funny boyish shoes and with the sunborn sweat soaking her eyes, she is part of the sky and earth, possibly a not too significant part, but a part. —TRUMAN CAPOTE

Any garden demands as much of its maker as he has to give. But I do not need to tell you, if you are a gardener, that no other undertaking will give as great a return for the amount of effort put into it. —ELIZABETH LAWRENCE

In England they have no sunlight or heat of a natural sunny sort, as indeed their gardeners are forever complaining. They make do—their gardens are the loveliest in the world today, largely because of the almost insurmountable challenge of the gray climate. There is nothing like impossibility for getting a gardener's energies up. Knowing that by nature they cannot (and do not) have anything, they have set themselves with zeal to the task of making gardens in the very face of the devil and the North Sea.

—HENRY MITCHELL

One afternoon, I found my wife kneeling at the edge of her perennial border on the north side, trying to disengage Achillea-the-Pearl from Coral Bell. "If I could afford it," she said bitterly, "I would take every damn bit of Achillea out of this border." She is a woman in comfortable circumstances, arrived at through her own hard labor, and this sudden burst of poverty, and her inability to indulge herself in a horticultural purge, startled me. I was so moved by her plight and her unhappiness that I went to the barn and returned with an edger, and we spent a fine, peaceable hour in the pretty twilight, rapping Achillea over the knuckles and saving Coral Bell.   —E. B. WHITE

There are no green thumbs or black thumbs. There are only gardeners and non-gardeners. Gardeners are the ones who ruin after ruin get on with the high defiance of nature herself, creating, in the very face of her chaos and tornado, the bower of roses and the pride of irises. It sounds very well to garden a "natural way." You may see the natural way in any desert, any swamp, any leech-filled laurel hell. Defiance, on the other hand, is what makes gardeners.

—HENRY MITCHELL

Thus to dream a garden and then to plant it is an act of independence and even defiance to the greater world. And though that garden or field you have first dreamed and then planted may later come in the high summer noon to seem a tyranny of its own, it is nonetheless one to which you have bound yourself voluntarily, with eyes open, head clear, without intermediary, without the slight of hand and the duplicity, or with much less of them, of human aggregations—political, corporate, whatever—that will always aspire to feed you, fuel your equipment, illuminate your nights, and imagine away your life.

—STANLEY CRAWFORD

To dig and delve in nice clean dirt
Can do a mortal little hurt.   —JOHN KENDRICK BANGS

Trench deep; dig in the rotting weeds;
Slash down the thistle's greybeard seeds;
Then make the frost your servant; make
His million fingers pry and break
The clods by glittering midnight stealth
Into the necessary tilth.

—VITA SACKVILLE-WEST

And he gave it for his opinion, that whoever could make two ears of corn to grow upon a spot of ground where only one grew before, would do more essential service to his country, than the whole race of politicians.

—JONATHAN SWIFT

I am always trying to induce vines to climb trees. A little studied negligence is becoming to a garden.

—ELEANOR PERENYI

I never had any other desire so strong and so like to covetousness, as that one which I have had always, that I might be master at last of a small house and a large garden.

—ABRAHAM COWLEY

Gardeners are much worse than fishermen—their arms stretch much wider when they are describing the height of their broad beans than when the fishermen are describing

the length of a pike, and their tongues run away with them
in a dreadful way, as though they were drunk with the
scent of the flowers they were describing.

—BEVERLEY NICHOLS

How I wish I had another 50 years to look forward to and
10 gardeners and 10 thousand pounds bequeathed to me
by a grateful shilling to be expended on nothing but the
garden.　　　　　　　　　—VITA SACKVILLE-WEST

I ask not for a larger garden,
But for finer seeds.　　　—RUSSELL HERMAN CONWELL

I know a little garden close,
Set thick with lily and red rose,
Where I would wander if I might
From dewy morn to dewy night.
　　　　　　　　　—WILLIAM MORRIS

What a man needs in gardening is a cast-iron back, with
a hinge in it.　　　　—CHARLES DUDLEY WARNER

"Might I," quavered Mary, "might I have a bit of earth?"
. . . Mr. Craven looked quite startled.
"Earth!" he repeated. "What do you mean?"
"To plant seeds in—to make things grow—to see them
come alive."
　　　　　　　　　—FRANCES HODGSON BURNETT

THE ANTI-GARDENER

I've had enough of gardening—I'm just about ready to throw in the trowel.

—ANONYMOUS

I would not say that every man should garden. Gardening does not come naturally to every man: we should not expect it of him, any more than expecting all men to be great lovers and all women mothers of children and good cooks.
—RICHARDSON WRIGHT

Airborne filth settling on aphis honeydew would asphyxiate all those plants which survive the sucking, biting, chewing, riddling activities of the insects, if it were not for the fact that they are generally pecked to death by sparrows, dug up, trodden on, sat on or stolen, or simply annihilated by a blast of animal urine or overwhelmed by a cloaking turd, long before that.   —ROSE BLIGHT (Germaine Greer)

I have a rock garden. Last week three of them died.
—RICHARD DIRAN

It is pure unadulterated country life. They get up early because they have so much to do and go to bed early because they have so little to think about. —OSCAR WILDE

Nothing grows in our garden, only washing. And babies.

—Dylan Thomas

Now, nature, as I am only too well aware, has her enthusiasts, but on the whole, I am not to be counted among them. To put it rather bluntly, I am not the type who wants to go back to the land; I am the type who wants to go back to the hotel.

—Fran Lebowitz

So *that's* what hay looks like.

—Queen Mary

Why is it no one ever sent me yet
One perfect limousine, do you suppose?
Ah no, it's always just my luck to get
One perfect rose.

—Dorothy Parker

A house is much more to my taste than a tree,
And for groves, oh! a good grove of chimneys for me.

—Charles Morris

THE ART
OF THE
GARDENER

*If you wish to make anything grow,
you must understand it in a very
real sense. "Green fingers" are a
fact, and a mystery only to the
unpracticed. But green fingers are
the extensions of a verdant heart.*

—RUSSELL PAGE

Gardening is a luxury occupation: an ornament, not a necessity, of life. The farmer is not at all concerned with the eventual beauty of his corn as a feature in the landscape, though, indeed, he gets a certain satisfaction out of it, as he leans against his gate on a summer evening, and sees his acres gently curving to the breeze. Still, beauty is not his primary aim; the gardener's is. Fortunate gardener, who may preoccupy himself solely with beauty in these difficult and ugly days! He is one of the few people left in this distressful world to carry on the tradition of elegance and charm. A useless member of society, considered in terms of economics, he must not be denied his rightful place. He deserves to share it, however humbly, with the painter and the poet. —VITA SACKVILLE-WEST

Strength may wield the ponderous spade,
May turn the clod, and wheel the compost home;
But elegance, chief grace the garden shows,
And most attractive, is the fair result
Of thought, the creature of a polished mind.
—WILLIAM COWPER

Gardeners and couturiers possess many of the same talents: imagination, knowledge, and industry. Both know which colors shock or coordinate, which textures rasp or soothe, and both see fashions change—but they never forget that the concept of beauty is timeless. —ROSEMARY VEREY

I farm—a kind of painting on earth, a kind of writing on earth—because of the constantly changing patterns I can create with water, seed, soil, sunlight, the weather. The memories of what I have made, the visions of what I hope to bring into existence, and the image of narrow channels of water winding their way through the back yards of my small valley: these are what most deeply motivate me.
—STANLEY CRAWFORD

I think there are as many kinds of gardening as of poetry.
—JOSEPH ADDISON

The life so short, the craft so long to learn. This was said about literature, but it really fits gardening better. Poetry, after all, is learned extremely early as a rule, if it is learned at all, but gardening is the province of old crocks past the age of twenty-eight. —HENRY MITCHELL

Nature in the garden is nature tamed, cultivated, made subservient to human purpose, brought into subjection to conscious purpose. A garden is not merely a piece of nature fenced in near the house, like a wolf chained at the back door; but nature cultivated and trained like a dog tamed and trained for human ends. Art in the garden is the human element appropriating and elevating the natural for human purpose. —ABRAM LINWOOD URBAN

Nature soon takes over if the gardener is absent.
—PENELOPE HOBHOUSE

Nature does not complete things. She is chaotic. Man must finish, and he does so by making a garden and building a wall. —ROBERT FROST

THE
CARELESS
GARDENER

*The nation that destroys
its soil destroys itself.*

—FRANKLIN D. ROOSEVELT

Never go to a doctor whose office plants have died.
—ERMA BOMBECK

Those that are wasters and willful spoilers of trees and plants, without just reason to do so, have seldom prospered in this world. —MOSES COOK

TOOLS

So deeply is the gardener's instinct
implanted in my soul, I really love the
tools with which I work—the iron
fork, the spade, the hoe, the rake, the
trowel, and the watering-pot are
pleasant objects in my eyes.

—CELIA THAXTER

Garden tools have a special meaning. They represent one of the great milestones in human evolution, when man began to grow his own food. The first tool was probably a pointed stick to scratch the earth and plant a seed, a revolutionary act that may mark the real beginning of civilization, the transition from hunter to farmer and the first settled communities. Then he learned to attach a shell or sharp stone to the stick and he had a primitive hoe and progress was on its way. —WILLIAM LONGGOOD

It is not one's partner's idleness or unfair apportionment of labour that may cut a marriage asunder, but it is wheelbarrows. Those lovely little three-legged objects which are the backbone of garden transport. No matter how many we have, and by now we have acquired four, they will be full, in the wrong place or mysteriously mislaid. They are the thin skin of garden compatibility, the Achilles' heel. Abuse, accusation and devious manipulation hang around wheelbarrows like bad vibes round the Moonies. Has any gardening couple ever owned enough wheelbarrows? I'd love to know. And if they have, what is the number?

—MIRABEL OSLER

Spade! with which Wilkinson hath tilled his lands,
And shaped these pleasant walks by Emont's side,
Thou art a tool of honor in my hands;
I press thee, through a yielding soil, with pride.
—WILLIAM WORDSWORTH

The green metal chair is an indispensable piece of equipment. As Farmer Bagley said, "How can you grow anything without a chair? How else you going to see what's going on?" —WILLIAM LONGGOOD

Those new to gardening should know, however, that most gardeners hate to part with dirt, clay pots, pickle jars, really good labels, stakes, tarred twine, and any kind of wooden box. They do not mind giving a plant that sells for $40 if they have an extra one, but the other stuff (which may be worth a dime) it tears the heart to part with. —HENRY MITCHELL

GARDEN ATTIRE

Unless you take care, the sun will pin you down. Put a hat on that foolish head of yours when you go out into the fields.

—FARMER'S ALMANAC

Gloves . . . interfered with the tactile pleasure of gardening.

—GAIL GODWIN

My wife had no garden clothes and never dressed for gardening. When she paid a call on her perennial borders or her cutting bed or her rose garden, she was not dressed for the part—she was simply a spur-of-the-moment escapee from the house and, in the early years, from the job of editing manuscripts. Her Army boots were likely to be Ferragamo shoes, and she wore no apron. I seldom saw her prepare for gardening, she merely wandered out into the cold and wet, into the sun and the warmth, wearing whatever she had put on that morning. Once she was drawn into the fray, once involved in transplanting or weeding or thinning or pulling deadheads, she forgot all else; her clothes had to take things as they came. . . . She simply refused to dress down to a garden: she moved in elegantly and walked among her flowers as she walked among her friends—nicely dressed, perfectly poised.

—E. B. WHITE

Come on! How often do you prune your Eugenia myrtifolia right after it blooms, the way Martha Stewart does, in December, wearing your lipstick? —ANNE RAVER

The person going out to plant wears gloves on her hands. She lifts out the first shovelful of earth and empties it to one side. It is neither wet nor hard, merely moist, easily poured. It contains air and well-made air channels and is therefore light in the way good bread sponge is light. Its fresh, earthy fragrance rises up, familiar and provocative; and suddenly the planter knows why she wore gloves. It was for the pleasure of shucking them off and taking a handful of the fresh earth up in her bare hands, to smell its satisfying perfume and feel it against her skin. Now is the moment for an intimate renewal of kinship with the earth. —RACHEL PEDEN

Don't wear perfume in the garden—unless you want to be pollinated by bees. —ANNE RAVER

WRITING ABOUT GARDENS

Any book about gardens, written for the pleasure of writing, must have its sources in dreams. The visions of gardens beautiful and retired hover before the imagination, and no real garden, however humble, but is invested in celestial light of cherished hopes of what it may become in fragrant flowers or what it might have been had fortune been kind.

—LENA MAY McCAULEY

❧ ❧ ❧

Almost everyone who grows things enjoys gardening books no matter how old-fashioned, for over and above the specific information they contain, they provide glimpses into a way of life that is not only gone forever but already in danger of being forgotten. —THALASSA CRUSO

I picked up a tattered copy of Alice Morse Earle's *Old-Time Gardens*. Because it was published in 1901, an "old time" itself, I thought it might be quaint and curious. It turned out to be about as quaint and curious as the Mozart *Requiem* or *The Cherry Orchard*, teaching the lesson that books on gardening, no less than musical and theatrical works, can be classics—not relics of the past, but fresh when discovered decades after their creator has gone to earth, and fresh on each new encounter. —ALLEN LACY

Garden notebooks are instant nostalgia, and sometimes they can make you feel a little sad for times long since past. But if you keep them going and never let them become a series of faded relics they will form a continuing microcosm of family history as well as an invaluable horticultural record. So do start one of your own, don't allow it to become a nuisance, and don't feel that it has to be fine literature; write in it when the spirit moves you. This way you will preserve for yourself, and perhaps for your children, a very pleasant account of how things were done by you and why.

—THALASSA CRUSO

Never dare tell me again anything about "green grass." Tell me how the lawn was flecked with shadows. I know perfectly well that grass is green. So does everybody else in England. . . . Make me see what it was that made your garden distinct from a thousand others.

—ROBERT LOUIS STEVENSON

PLEASURES
AND
SATISFACTIONS

Yes! in the poor man's garden grow,
  Far more than herbs and flowers,
Kind thoughts, contentment, peace of
    mind,
  And joy for weary hours.

—MARY HOWITT

It is curious, pathetic almost, how deeply seated in the human heart is the liking for gardens and gardening.

—ALEXANDER SMITH

Who loves a garden still his Eden keeps,
Perennial pleasures plants, and wholesome harvest reaps.

—AMOS BRONSON ALCOTT

I have often thought that if heaven had given me a choice of my position and calling, it should have been on a rich spot of earth, well watered, and near a good market for the productions of the garden. No occupation is so delightful to me as the culture of the earth, and no culture comparable to that of the garden. Such a variety of subjects, some one always coming to perfection, the failure of one thing repaired by the success of another, and instead of one harvest a continued one through the year. Under a total want of demand except for our family table, I am still devoted to the garden. But though an old man, I am but a young gardener.

—THOMAS JEFFERSON

Letter to Vita Sackville-West, 24 April 1951:

What a perfect day it was yesterday, the pale stream of the River Thames was gilded by the strangest alchemy and all the willows were bursting into green: I sat in my tower [Windsor Castle] looking out towards the Chilterns and thought of our lovely garden all green and yellow and expectant. It is, is, is a lovely garden and I was so happy on Sunday just walking with you among the loveliness you made. I think it is the loveliest garden in the whole world.

—HAROLD NICOLSON

Not useless are ye flowers; though made for pleasure,
Blooming o'er fields, and wave by day and night
From every source your sanction bids me treasure
Harmless delight.

—HORACE SMITH

One of the small delights of gardening, undramatic but recurring, is when phlox or columbines seed themselves in unplanned places. —MIRABEL OSLER

One should learn also to enjoy the neighbor's garden, however small; the roses straggling over the fence, the scent of lilacs drifting across the road. —HENRY VAN DYKE

The lesson I have thoroughly learnt, and wish to pass on to others, is to know the enduring happiness that the love of a garden gives. I rejoice when I see anyone, and espe-cially children, inquiring about flowers, and wanting gar-dens of their own, and carefully working in them. For love of gardening is a seed that once sown never dies, but always grows and grows to an enduring and ever-increasing source of happiness.   —GERTRUDE JEKYLL

What I do know is that few satisfactions match having grown-up children who obviously share my belief that dig-ging in the earth has, since Eden, been the best way of staying out of trouble and meanwhile experiencing sensual delights that beggar my powers of description.
                                                    —ALLEN LACY

The main purpose of a garden is to give its owner the best and highest kind of earthly pleasure.
                                                —GERTRUDE JEKYLL

The works of a person that builds begin immediately to decay; while those of him who plants begin directly to improve. In this, planting promises a more lasting pleasure than building.   —WILLIAM SHENSTONE

There is nothing pleasanter than spading when the ground is soft and damp.   —JOHN STEINBECK

This little space which scented box encloses
Is blue with lupins and is sweet with thyme
My garden all is overblown with roses,
My spirit all is overblown with rhyme,
As like a drunken honeybee I waver
From house to garden and again to house,
And, undetermined which delight to favour,
On verse and rose alternatively carouse.
—VITA SACKVILLE-WEST

Through primrose tufts, in that green bower,
The periwinkle trailed its wreaths;
And 'tis my faith that every flower
Enjoys the air it breathes.

The budding twigs spread out their fan
To catch the breezy air;
And I must think, do all I can,
That there was pleasure there.
—WORDSWORTH

To take a spade or a spading fork on a crisp fall day and
without undue haste or backbreaking effort to turn over
slice after slice of sweet-smelling earth can bring rich rewards to the gardener who fully understands just what he
is accomplishing.   —T. H. EVERETT

But a little garden, the littler the better, is your richest chance for happiness and success.   —REGINALD FARRER

He who plants a garden, plants happiness.

—CHINESE PROVERB

In all the recipes for happiness I have ever seen, "something to look forward to" has been given as an important ingredient. Something to look forward to! How rich the gardener, any gardener, is in this particular integrant! For always he looks forward to something if it is only the appearance of the red noses of the Peonies in the spring or the sharp aromas that fills the air in autumn after the frost has touched the herbage.   —LOUISE BEEBE WILDER

The man who has planted a garden feels that he has done something for the good of the whole world.
—CHARLES DUDLEY WARNER

The joy of being able to cut flowers freely, lavishly, to decorate the house and to give to friends is an end that justifies a lot of gardening effort. —T. H. EVERETT

Then I went out for two hours late in the afternoon and put in a hundred tulips. In itself that would not be a big job, but everywhere I have to clear space for them, weed, divide perennials, rescue iris that is being choked by violets. I really get to weeding only in the spring and autumn, so I am working through a jungle now. Doing it I feel strenuously happy and at peace. At the end of the afternoon on a gray day, the light is sad and one feels the chill, but the bitter smell of earth is a tonic. —MAY SARTON

To own a bit of ground, to scratch it with a hoe, to plant seeds, and watch their renewal of life, this is the commonest delight of the race, the most satisfactory thing a man can do. —CHARLES DUDLEY WARNER

What I enjoy is not the fruits alone, but I also enjoy the soil itself, its nature and its power. —CICERO

When I walk out of my house into my garden I walk out of my habitual self, my every-day thoughts, my customariness of joy and sorrow by which I recognise and assure myself of my own identity. These I leave behind me for a time, as the bather leaves his garments on the beach. —ALEXANDER SMITH

Working in the garden ... gives me a profound feeling of inner peace. Nothing here is in a hurry. There is no rush toward accomplishment, no blowing of trumpets. Here is the great mystery of life and growth. Everything is changing, growing, aiming at something, but silently, unboastfully, taking its time. —RUTH STOUT

A morning-glory at my window satisfies me more than the metaphysics of books. —WALT WHITMAN

No occupation is so delightful to me as the culture of the earth. —THOMAS JEFFERSON

*Arranging a bowl of flowers in the
morning can give a sense of quiet
in a crowded day—like writing a
poem or saying a prayer.*
—ANNE MORROW LINDBERGH

But she gladly sacrificed a very beautiful flower to a very small
child, a child not yet able to speak, like the little boy whom a
neighbor to the east proudly brought into the garden one day,
to show him off to her. My mother found fault with the infant's
swaddling clothes, for being too tight, untied his three-piece
bonnet and his unnecessary woolen shawl, and then gazed to
her heart's content on his bronze ringlets, his cheeks, and the
enormous, stern black eyes of a ten months' old baby boy. . . .
She gave him a cuisse-de-nymphe-emue rose, and he accepted
it with delight, put it in his mouth, and sucked it; then he
kneaded it with his powerful little hands and tore off the petals,
as curved and carmine as his own lips.   —COLETTE

If you can get hold of a branch [of mulberry] from someone
else's tree, and put it into the ground, it will grow. Just as
the willow tree does—but far more slowly. Give a mulberry
tree for a wedding present, if they seem like a staying
couple.   —JANE GRIGSON

He who offers violets must in love be held to offer roses. Of all the fragrant herbs I send, none can compare in nobleness with the purple violet. —FORTUNATUS

I knew when I walked in here last Sunday that this house dies when there are no flowers. It felt desolate and I ended the day in tears, as if I had been abandoned by God. Now there are crimson tulips in one room, white and pink ones in another, and I can breathe, am full of joy and at home again. —MAY SARTON

I would have taken care of daisies, giving them aspirin every hour and cutting their stems properly, but with roses I'm reckless. When they arrive in their long white box, they're already in the death house. —ANNE SEXTON

I'd rather have roses on my table than diamonds on my neck. —EMMA GOLDMAN

Flowers leave some of their fragrance in the hand that bestows them.
—CHINESE PROVERB

And after all the weather was ideal! They could not have had a more perfect day for a garden-party if they had ordered it. Windless, warm, the sky without a cloud. Only the blue was veiled with a haze of light gold, as it is sometimes in early summer. The gardener had been up since dawn, mowing the lawns and sweeping them, until the grass and the dark flat rosettes where the daisy plants had been seemed to shine. As for the roses, you could not help feeling they understood that roses are the only flowers that impress people at garden parties; the only flowers that everyone is certain of knowing. Hundreds, yes, literally hundreds, had come out in a single night; the green bushes bowed down as though they had been visited by archangels.
—KATHERINE MANSFIELD

Hoeing in the garden on a bright, soft May day, when you are not obliged to, is nearly equal to the delight of going trouting.　　　　　　—CHARLES DUDLEY WARNER

Watering my garden late on a soft summer night in the empty French countryside was a rapturous experience. As the moon led me, I walked back and forth to the bank near the stream, threw my bucket in, and hauled up bucket after bucket of cool water from the stream. I couldn't see the stream, or the bucket when it landed, but I could hear the splash. Once they got used to me, the frogs continued their mad barking and gave me my metronome. . . . Being at my garden so late, guided only by the light of the moon, was like working in a pale, white sea, and my motions, somewhat tentative and groping, made me feel as if I were swimming in the night.   —RICHARD GOODMAN

It was the reflected glow of your blazing line along the terrace, O geraniums, and yours, O foxgloves, springing up amid the coppice, that gave my childish cheeks their rosy warmth.   —COLETTE

A dear neighbor brought me a tussie-mussie this week. The dictionary defines tuzzy-muzzy, or tussie-mussie, as "a bunch or posy of flowers, a nosegay," and then disobligingly adds that the word is obsolete. I refuse to regard it as obsolete. It is a charming word; I have always used it and shall continue to use it, whatever the great Oxford Dictionary may say.   —VITA SACKVILLE-WEST

I personally like manure. I never feel so affluent as when bringing back the occasional load of high-class dung. When we moved here and I was preparing the new garden, Stu brought a pickup load of horse manure as a garden-warming present. I never had a more welcome or thoughtful gift.   —WILLIAM LONGGOOD

No poet I've ever heard of has written an ode to a load of manure. Somebody should, and I'm not trying to be funny.   —RUTH STOUT

One of the most endearing qualities of gardeners, though it makes their gardens worse, is this faculty of being too easily delighted.   —HENRY MITCHELL

What a delight it is
When, of a morning,
I get up and go out
To find in full bloom a flower
That yesterday was not there.
                    —TACHIBANA AKEMI

INSPIRATION
AND
IMAGINATION

For oft, when on my couch I lie
In vacant or in pensive mood,
They flash upon the inward eye
Which is the bliss of solitude;
And then my heart with pleasure fills,
And dances with the daffodils.

—WILLIAM WORDSWORTH

I have never had so many good ideas day after day as when I work in the garden. —JOHN ERSKINE

In my garden there is a large place for sentiment. My garden of flowers is also my garden of thoughts and dreams. The thoughts grow as freely as the flowers, and the dreams are as beautiful. —ABRAM LINWOOD URBAN

The eighteenth-century view of the garden was that it should lead the observer to the enjoyment of the aesthetic sentiments of regularity and order, proportion, color and utility, and furthermore, be capable of arousing feelings of grandeur, gaiety, sadness, wildness, domesticity, surprise and secrecy. —PENELOPE HOBHOUSE

The only limit to your garden is at the boundaries of your imagination. —THOMAS D. CHURCH

A garden is to be enjoyed, and should satisfy the mind and not only the eye of the beholder. Sounds such as the rustle of bamboo and the dripping of water, scents and sensations such as grass or gravel or stone underfoot, appeal to the emotions and play a part in the total impression. —PENELOPE HOBHOUSE

HEARTBREAKS AND LAMENTS

Before they bloomed I longed for them;
  After they bloomed, I mourned that
    they must fade;
The mountain cherry-flowers
  Sorrow alone for my poor heart have
    made.

—NAKATSUKASA

❧ ❧ ❧

Wherever humans garden magnificently, there are magnificent heartbreaks. It may be forty heifers break through the hedge after a spring shower and (undiscovered for many hours) trample the labor of many years into uniform mire. It may be the gardener has nursed along his camellias for twenty-five years, and in one night of February they are dead. How can that be? Well, it can be.

—HENRY MITCHELL

A killing frost devastates the heart as well as the garden.

—ELEANOR PERENYI

If "heartache" sounds exaggerated then surely you have never gone to your garden one rare morning in June to find that the frost, without any perceptible motive, any hope of personal gain, has quietly killed your strawberry blossoms, tomatoes, lima and green beans, corn, squash, cucumbers. A brilliant sun is now smiling at this disaster with an insensitive cheerfulness as out of place as a funny story would be if someone you loved had just died.

—RUTH STOUT

As I write this, on June 29, its time for another summer storm to smash the garden to pieces, though it may hold off until the phlox, tomatoes, daylilies, and zinnias are in full sway.   —HENRY MITCHELL

For I do believe that flowers have feelings, and that those feelings extend to the human being who tends them. . . . By no other theory can I explain, for example, my own total failure to grow alstroemerias, the lovely Peruvian lilies that flower in July. On the packet—or rather the bulb bag—it tells you that "they resent lime." Not a speck of lime did they get. It wasn't lime they resented, it was me. Again, it said that they "succeed best in half shade." They got it, but they didn't succeed; my own shadow had fallen across them. In desperation I bought them in pots, planted them already established. But they died down and never came up again. "Death," they obviously said to themselves, "is better than the thought of seeing that face again."
                                        —BEVERLEY NICHOLS

The doctor can bury his mistakes but an architect can only advise his client to plant vines. —FRANK LLOYD WRIGHT

I often thought the whole world would not sleep o' nights if it knew by what perilous margin the food supply was wangled out of the stubborn earth.
                                —KATHERINE ANNE PORTER

Horticulturally speaking I must, I think, be the lineal descendant of Jonah as well as Job, for disaster and foul weather always seem to haunt any garden occasion with which I may be associated.   —THALASSA CRUSO

As a matter of fact, you know I am rather sorry you should see the garden now, because, alas! it is not looking at its best. Oh, it doesn't *compare* to what it was last year.
—RUTH DRAPER

But ne'er the rose without the thorn.   —ROBERT HERRICK

Each year, upon returning to my garden again, the same dismay: disappearance of the rare species and varieties; triumph of the common and mediocre ones.
—ANDRE GIDE

I am suffering from my old complaint, the hayfever. My fear is, perishing by deliquescence; I melt away in nasal and lachrymal profluvia. My remedies are warm pediluvium, cathartics, topical application of a watery solution of opium to eyes, ears, and the interior of the nostrils. The membrance is so irritable that light, dust, contradiction, an absurd remark, the sight of a Dissenter—anything, sets me sneezing.   —SYDNEY SMITH

I don't know if I cotton to weekend gardening. Growing plants without being there is like having a baby and letting somebody else take care of it. —ANNE RAVER

*L*ast night, there came a frost, which has done great damage to my garden. . . . It is sad that Nature will play such tricks with us poor mortals, inviting us with sunny smiles to confide in her, and then, when we are entirely within her power, striking us to the heart.

—NATHANIEL HAWTHORNE

Man . . . is fighting a lone fight against vast indifference. A gardener learns that. His flowers are fighting the same sort of lone fight, and perhaps that is why he loves them and pities them. —WARWICK DEEPING

The kiss of the wind for lumbago,
The stab of the thorn for mirth,
One is nearer to death in the garden
Than anywhere else on earth.

—ELEANOR PERENYI

There's nothing like the impending visit of a critical gardening relative for forcing the cold, hard horticultural deficiencies of your own yard upon you. —THALASSA CRUSO

You're supposed to get tired planting bulbs. But it's an agreeable tiredness.   —GAIL GODWIN

Summer in the Garden

*The late summer garden has a tranquility
found no other time of year.*

—William Longgood

The serene philosophy of the pink rose is steadying. Its fragrant, delicate petals open fully and are ready to fall, without regret or disillusion, after only a day in the sun. It is so every summer. One can almost hear their pink, fragrant murmur as they settle down upon the grass: "Summer, summer, it will always be summer."   —RACHEL PEDEN

> Sumer is icumen in,
>   Lhude sing cuccu.
> Groweth sed, and bloweth med,
>   And springth the wude nu,
> Sing cuccu!
>   —ANONYMOUS

The flowers are nature's jewels, with whose wealth she decks her summer beauty.   —GEORGE CROLY

Summer set lip to earth's bosom bare
And left the flushed print in a poppy there.
                                   —FRANCIS THOMPSON

'Long about knee-deep in June,
'Bout the time strawberries melts
On the vine.

         —JAMES WHITCOMB RILEY

Hot July brings cooling showers,
Apricots and gillyflowers.

         —SARA COLERIDGE

Not wholly in the busy world, nor quite
Beyond it, blooms the garden that I love.
News from the humming city comes to it
It sounds of funeral or of marriage bells.

         —ALFRED, LORD TENNYSON

Dry August and warm,
Doth harvest no harm.

         —THOMAS TUSSER

In August, the large masses of berries, which, when in
flower, had attracted many wild bees, gradually assumed
their bright velvety crimson hue, and by their weight again
bent down and broke their tender limbs.

         —HENRY DAVID THOREAU

The brilliant poppy flaunts her head
Amidst the ripening grain,
And adds her voice to swell the song
That August's here again.

—HELEN WINSLOW

It is a sad moment when the first phlox appears. It is the amber light indicating the end of the great burst of early summer and suggesting that we must now start looking forward to autumn. Not that I have any objection to autumn as a season, full of its own beauty; but I just cannot bear to see another summer go, and I recoil from what the first hint of autumn means.   —VITA SACKVILLE-WEST

Along the river's summer walk,
The withered tufts of asters nod;
And trembles on its arid stalk
The hoar plume of the golden-rod.

—JOHN GREENLEAF WHITTIER

Those were summers when the heart quivered up from the hot yellow gravel and pierced the plaited rushes of my wide-brimmed hats, summers almost without nights. For even

then I so loved the dawn that my mother granted it to me as a reward. She used to agree to wake me at half past three and off I would go, an empty basket on each arm, toward the kitchen gardens that sheltered in the narrow bend of the river, in search of strawberries, black currants, and hairy gooseberries.   —COLETTE

Winter is cold-hearted,
Spring is yea and nay,
Autumn is a weather cock
Blown every way.
Summer days for me
When every leaf is on its tree.
                    —CHRISTINA ROSSETTI

'Tis the last rose of summer,
Left blooming alone;
All her lovely companions
Are faded and gone.
—THOMAS MOORE

Summer afternoon—summer afternoon; to me those have always been the two most beautiful words in the English language.   —HENRY JAMES

THE SENSUAL
GARDEN

*The greatest gift of a garden is the
restoration of the five senses.*

—HANNA RION

C

O the green things growing, the green things growing,
The faint sweet smell of the green things growing!
—DINAH MULOCK CRAIK

Flowers really do intoxicate me. —VITA SACKVILLE-WEST

Fresh spring the herald of love's mighty king,
In whose coat armour richly are display'd
All sorts of flowers which on earth do spring
In goodly colours gloriously array'd.
—EDMUND SPENSER

How can one help shivering with delight when one's hot
fingers close around the stem of a live flower, cool from
the shade and stiff with newborn vigor.   —COLETTE

An apple tree does not have to justify its existence by
bearing fruit. Its fragrance, so delicate that it is almost
stronger in memory than in reality, is sufficient. Or the
sight of it. Irresistibly you step close enough to inhale from
the heart of one bloom, although actually the fragrance is

more distinct if you stand back a few steps letting the sun-touched wind bring the perfume to you. No one can ever forget the smell or the sight of a wide-spreading apple tree in full bloom. —RACHEL PEDEN

I am in love with the green earth. —CHARLES LAMB

> Annihilating all that's made
> To a green thought in a green shade.
> —ANDREW MARVELL

At the center of each man's being, says Chesterton, is a dream. My pet dream for many years has been a white garden, set apart and inclosed within a shining green hedge.
—LOUISE BEEBE WILDER

> Blue thou art, intensely blue!
> Flower! whence came thy dazzling hue?
> When I opened first mine eye,
> Upward glancing at the sky,
> Straightway from the firmament
> Was the sapphire brilliance sent.
> —JAMES MONTGOMERY

For my own part, I am trying to make a grey, green, and white garden. This is an experiment which I ardently hope may be successful, though I doubt it. . . . All the same, I cannot help hoping that the great ghostly barn owl will sweep silently across a pale garden, next summer, in the twilight—the pale garden that I am now planting, under the first flakes of snow.   —VITA SACKVILLE-WEST

Green is the fresh emblem of well-founded hopes. In blue the spirit can wander, but in green it can rest.
—MARY WEBB

He wanted a flower garden of yellow daisies because they were the only flower which resembled the face of his wife and the sun of his love.   —BESSIE HEAD

Last summer I was staying at a house in Hampshire which was famous for the brilliance and the originality of its gardens. There were many of them, but the most beautiful of all was a walled garden in which every flower was blue. There were all the obvious things like delphiniums and aconitums and larkspurs, but the most beautiful blue of all came from groups of cabbages—the ordinary blue pickling cabbage. Set against the blazing blue of the other flowers, it had a bloom and an elegance which made it a thing of the greatest delight.   —BEVERLEY NICHOLS

No white nor red was ever seen
So amorous as this lovely green.
                    —ANDREW MARVELL

Verde que te quiero verde,
Verde viento. Verde ramas.
Green how I love you green.
Green wind. Green branches.
                    —FEDERICO GARCÍA LORCA

And I will make thee beds of roses,
And a thousand fragrant posies.
                    —CHRISTOPHER MARLOWE

Come into the garden, Maud,
For the black bat, night, has flown;
Come into the garden, Maud,
I am here at the gate alone;
And the woodbine spices are wafted abroad,
And the musk of the rose is blown.
                    —ALFRED, LORD TENNYSON

In one way or another Eros operates in every garden.

—MICHAEL POLLAN

It was not in the winter
Our loving lot was cast!
It was the time of roses,
We plucked them as we passed!

—THOMAS HOOD

I took my adorable girl to all those secret spots in the woods, where I had daydreamed so ardently of meeting her, of creating her. In one particular pine grove everything fell into place, I parted the fabric of fancy, I tasted reality. As my uncle was absent that year, we could also stray freely in his huge, dense, two-century-old park with its classical cripples of green-stained stone in the main avenue and labyrinthine paths radiating from a central fountain. We walked "swinging hands," country-fashion. I picked dahlias for her on the borders along the gravel drive.

—VLADIMIR NABOKOV

O, my Luve is like a red, red rose,
That's newly sprung in June.   —ROBERT BURNS

When a young man presents a tulip to his mistress he gives her to understand, by the general colour of the flower, that he is on fire with her beauty, and by the black base of it his heart is burnt to a coal.   —SIR JOHN CHARDIN

One heard the musical voice of the garden, whose loveliest hours revealed their joyous soul and sang of their gladness. —MAURICE MAETERLINCK

The musicians are in excellent form tonight. The company is made up of crickets, katydids, cicadas, grasshoppers, and others, perhaps, that I do not recognize. Artists all! Already they have tuned up. The maestro has given the downbeat. The program is under way with a scraping of ridged wings and file-like legs, a resonance of clicks, buzzes, chirps, and trills. They saw and rasp away, the sounds amplified and vibrating in insect bodies on the night air. The faster the tempo, the higher the pitch. I have read that the insect song is in the key of C-sharp but some say it is more varied. I would not know.   —WILLIAM LONGGOOD

Drunk on roses, I look round and wonder which to recommend.
—VITA SACKVILLE-WEST

The morning rose that untouch'd stands
Arm'd with her briers, how sweet she smells!
But pluck'd and strain'd through ruder hands,
Her sweets no longer with her dwells.

—SIR ROBERT AYTOUN

It grew late. Through the open door, stealthily, came the scent of madonna lilies, almost as if it were prowling abroad. —D. H. LAWRENCE

A garden full of sweet odours is a garden full of charm, a most precious kind of charm not to be implanted by mere skill in horticulture or power of purse, and which is beyond explaining. It is born of sensitive and very personal preferences yet its appeal is almost universal.

—LOUISE BEEBE WILDER

And because the breath of flowers is far sweeter in the air (where it comes and goes, like the warbling of music) than in the hand, therefore nothing is more fit for that delight than to know what be the flowers and plants that do best perfume the air. —FRANCIS BACON

And then, like a shock, he caught another perfume, something raw and coarse. Hunting round, he found the purple iris, touched their fleshy throats and their dark, grasping hands. At any rate, he had found something. They stood stiff in the darkness. Their scent was brutal. The moon was melting down upon the crest of the hill. It was gone; all was dark. —D. H. LAWRENCE

And there came a smell off the Shore like the Smell of a Garden. —JOHN WINTHROP

When I take the kitchen middens from the latest canning session out to the compost before going to bed, the orchestra is in full chorus. Night vapors and scents from the earth mingle with the fragrance of honeysuckle nearby and basil growing in the compost. They merge into the rhythmic pulse of night. —WILLIAM LONGGOOD

I hope I do not ruin this letter for you by enclosing a little vetivert; add this to the smells in the street. It is all Louisiana in a little dried herb. It is good for putting among linen, and if you like I shall send you some for Stoneblossom. If you do not care for it, say so surely, otherwise you will be getting a bale of it. I hung a little bunch in a window for the wind to blow through, and wonder how on earth I could have forgotten it, of all things, when I remembered this place.   —KATHERINE ANNE PORTER

Let's go to the house, for the linen looks white, and smells of lavender, and I long to lie in a pair of sheets that smell so.   —IZAAK WALTON

Many herbes and flowers with their fragrant sweet smels doe comfort, and as it were revive the spirits and perfume the whole house.

—JOHN PARKINSON

❧ ❧ ❧

Of all the ingredients we employ in the creation of a garden, scent is probably the most potent and the least understood. Its effects can be either direct and immediate, drowning our senses in a surge of sugary vapour, or they can be subtle and delayed, slowly wafting into our consciousness, stirring our emotions and colouring our thoughts.   —STEPHEN LACEY

Oh, how much more doth beauty beauteous seem
By that sweet ornament which truth doth give!
The rose looks fair, but fairer we it deem
For that sweet odour which doth in it live.
—WILLIAM SHAKESPEARE

Scents bring memories, and many memories bring nostalgic
pleasure. We would be wise to plan for this when we plant
a garden.   —THALASSA CRUSO

The delicate odour of Mignonette,
    The reamins of a dead and gone bouquet,
Is all that tells of a story; yet
    Could we think of it in a sweeter way?
—BRET HARTE

The flower of sweetest smell is shy and lowly.
—WILLIAM WORDSWORTH

The fragrance always remains in the hand that gives the
rose.   —HEDA BEJAR

The gardens of my youth were fragrant gardens and it is
their sweetness rather than their patterns or their furnish-
ings that I now most clearly recall.
—LOUISE BEEBE WILDER

The rose has one powerful virtue to boast
Above all the flowers of the field:
When its leaves are all dead, and fine colours are lost,
Still how sweet a perfume
It will yield!

—ISAAC WATTS

The rose looks fair, but fairer we it deem
For that sweet odor which doth in it live.

—WILLIAM SHAKESPEARE

The strange thing which I have experienced with flower scents, and indeed with all other scents, is that they only recall pleasant memories.   —THEODORE A. STEPHENS

Then will I raise aloft the milk-white Rose,
With whose sweet smell the air shall be perfumed.

—WILLIAM SHAKESPEARE

They walked over the crackling leaves in the garden, between the lines of Box, breathing its fragrance of eternity; for this is one of the odors which carry us out of time into the abysses of the unbeginning past; if we ever lived on another ball of stone than this, it must be that there was Box growing on it.   —OLIVER WENDELL HOLMES

Those [herbs] which perfume the air most delightfully, not passed by as the rest, but, being trodden upon and crushed, are three; that is, burnet, wild thyme and watermints. Therefore, you are to set whole alleys of them, to have the pleasure when you walk or tread.   —FRANCIS BACON

Through the open door
A drowsy smell of flowers—gray
*   heliotrope*
And white sweet clover, and shy
*   mignonette*
Comes fairly in, and silent chorus
*   leads*
To the pervading symphony of Peace.
   —JOHN GREENLEAF WHITTIER

When I was a boy, I thought scent was contained in dew-drops on flowers and if I got up very early in the morning, I could collect it and make perfume.
   —OSCAR DE LA RENTA

With the smell of iris and budding acacia coming through the windows, the sound of scholasticism filling my dreams with a reassuring hum, I sank deeper and deeper into a kind of cerebral miasma as I postponed all vital decisions.

—AGNES DE MILLE

There are few pleasures like really burrowing one's nose into sweet peas. —ANGELA THIRKELL

That which above all other yields the sweetest smell in the air is the violet. —FRANCIS BACON

TREES IN THE GARDEN

*He that plants trees loves others
besides himself.*

—THOMAS FULLER

It is in winter that trees reveal what they most truly are—alien presences possessed of a stark and foreign beauty that owes little to the human race. In this season, I come to understand the reasons the Druids among my ancestors had for giving them worship. In other seasons we may almost deceive ourselves into believing that trees exist for our purposes, that they are extensions of ourselves, meant to serve our wants and needs. In early spring, when the willow twigs change from yellow-gold to pale green, we find a metaphor of hope for a world made new. In summer we find refreshment in their cool green shade. In autumn they so dazzle the eye that we forget the approach of winter's harshness. And in their deaths, trees serve us in myriad useful ways, giving us fuel and shelter, pencils and paper, ax handles and broomsticks. —ALLEN LACY

. . . our favorite birch tree. It was yielding to the gusty wind with all its tender twigs, the sun shone upon it and it glanced in the wind like a flying sunshiny tower. It was a tree in shape with stem and branches but it was like a Spirit of water. . . . The other birch trees that were near it looked bright and cheerful, but it was a creature by its own self among them. —DOROTHY WORDSWORTH

The birch, most shy and ladylike of trees.
—JAMES RUSSELL LOWELL

A man does not plant a tree for himself; he plants it for posterity. —ALEXANDER SMITH

A solitary maple on a woodside flames in single scarlet, recalls nothing so much as the daughter of a noble house dressed for a fancy ball, with the whole family gathered round to admire her before she goes.

—HENRY JAMES

A stricken tree, a living thing, so beautiful, so dignified, so admirable in its potential longevity, is, next to man, perhaps the most touching of wounded objects.
—EDNA FERBER

A tree is a tree—how many more do you need to look at?
—RONALD REAGAN

An apple-tree puts to shame all the men and women that
have attempted to dress since the world began.
—H. W. BEECHER

Except during the nine months before he draws his first
breath, no man manages his affairs as well as a tree does.
—GEORGE BERNARD SHAW

Generations pass while some tree stands, and old families
last not three oaks.   —SIR THOMAS BROWNE

The tree man stood in the garden and complained . . .
against modern life, which he says, is anti-tree.
  "Every day," he said, bitter, bitter: "they ring. I go.
There's a fine tree. It's taken a hundred years to grow—
what are we, compared to a tree? They say, cut it, it's
spoiling my roses. Roses! What are roses, compared to a
tree? I have to cut a tree for the sake of the roses. Only
yesterday I had to cut an ash down to three feet off the
ground. To make a table, *she* said, a table, and the tree
took a hundred years to grow. She wanted to sit at a table

and drink her tea and look at her roses. No trees these days, the trees are going. And if you do a good job, they don't like it, no, they want it hacked out of real shape. And what about the birds? Did you know you had a nest up on that branch?" —DORIS LESSING

I don't know when tree houses for adults went out of fashion—and still less why. I myself would rather have an arboreal retreat than a swimming pool any day.
—ELEANOR PERENYI

I like trees because they seem more resigned to the way they have to live than other things do. —WILLA CATHER

I never before knew the full value of trees. My house is entirely embosomed in high plane trees, with good grass below, and under them I breakfast, dine, write, read and receive my company. What would I not give that the trees planted nearest round the house at Monticello were full grown. —THOMAS JEFFERSON

Plants are the young of the world, vessels of health and vigor; but they grope ever upward towards consciousness; the trees are imperfect men, and seem to bemoan their imprisonment, rooted in the ground.

—RALPH WALDO EMERSON

I thank you for the seeds. . . . Too old to plant trees for my own gratification, I shall do it for my posterity.

—THOMAS JEFFERSON

It is worth any amount of effort to be able to see your house through the arch of a tree. —THOMAS D. CHURCH

Loveliest of trees, the cherry now
Is hung with bloom along the bough,
And stands about the woodland ride
Wearing white for Eastertide.

—A. E. HOUSMAN

Of all man's works of art, a cathedral is greatest. A vast and majestic tree is greater than that. —H. W. BEECHER

[Trees] hang on from a past no theory can recover. They will survive us. The air makes their music. Otherwise they live in savage silence, though mites and nematodes and spiders teem at their roots, and though the energy with which they feed on the sun and are able to draw water sometimes hundreds of feet up their trunks and into their twigs and branches calls for a deafening volume of sound.

—JOHN HAY

Together with a few human beings, dead and living, and their achievements, trees are what I most love and revere.

—HILDEGARD FLANNER

Trees come out of acorns, no matter how unlikely that seems. An acorn is just a tree's way back into the ground. For another try. Another trip through. One life for another.

—SHIRLEY ANN GRAU

While trees are excellent for apes, owls, and arboreal fauna in general, they are annoying in a small garden where one hopes to grow something besides a compost pile and a continental championship collection of slugs and sowbugs.

—HENRY MITCHELL

A song to the oak, the brave old oak,
  Who hath ruled in the greenwood long;
Here's health and renown to his broad green crown,
  And his fifty arms so strong.

—H. F. CHORLEY

There is in trees no perfect form which can be reasoned out as ideal; but that is always an ideal oak which, however poverty-stricken, or hunger-pinched, or tempest tortured, is yet seen to have done, under its appointed circumstances, all that could be expected of oak.   —JOHN RUSKIN

A double row of huge old poplars beside the narrow brook swayed and danced in the gales, rustled in the late spring breeze, stood spirelike heavy in July sunlight.

—RICHARD ALDINGTON

LABORS

Gardens are not made,
By singing—"Oh, how beautiful!"
and sitting in the shade.

—RUDYARD KIPLING

When I go into my garden with a spade, and dig a bed, I feel such an exhilaration and health that I discover that I have been defrauding myself all this time in letting others do for me what I should have done with my own hands.

—RALPH WALDO EMERSON

Through the window one could see kerchiefed peasant girls weeding a garden path on their hands and knees or gently raking the sun-mottled sand.   —VLADIMIR NABOKOV

Fall—not spring—is the great planting season for woody things. If, in other words, you had thought of lolling in the warm weekends admiring the chrysanthemums and the dogwoods turning red, congratulating yourself perhaps that the weeds are losing heart, let me cheerfully remind you that you should be exhausted (not lolling) since this is the busiest of all garden seasons. When you are not planting bulbs, digging up bindweed roots, rooting out pokeweed, soaking bamboo, there are still other tasks. Thousands of them. You are terribly behind. The very idea of just sitting about in the sun!   —HENRY MITCHELL

I wanted no one lifting a finger in that garden unless he loved doing it. What if Fred had hired a man to dig those trenches and it had turned out that he didn't love to dig? Who would eat that kind of asparagus?   —RUTH STOUT

How stuffy of Kipling. How priggish, and anyway, why not? Surely ruminating and lolling, squandering slivers of time as you ponder on this or that plant; perching about the place on seats chosen for their essential and individual quality, are other whole aspects of being a gardener. Why shouldn't we? We sit in other people's gardens, why not in our own?   —MIRABEL OSLER

A fallow field is a sin.
—JOHN STEINBECK

❧ ❧ ❧

I'm tired of hearing so much about maintenance-free gardens. If you aren't going to get out there and live with it—including taking care of it—then what's the point of gardening anyway? This year I'm going to order fewer new things and concentrate on taking care of what I have.
—PAMELA LORD

Man was not made to rust out in idleness. A degree of exercise is as necessary for the preservation of health, both of body and mind, as his daily food. And what exercise is more fitting, or more appropriate for one who is in the decline of life, than that of superintending a well-ordered garden? What more enlivens the sinking mind? What is more conducive to a long life?

—JOSEPH BRECK

Nothing known to man equals a rock garden for labor. Incredibly enough, I have twice seen rock gardens advocated as labor-saving devices, but this only proves that human perversity is boundless.   —HENRY MITCHELL

You cannot plough a field by turning it over in your mind.

—ANONYMOUS

The garden cost Amelia no end of work and worry; she tended the delicate tomato vines as though they were new born infants, and suffered momentary sinking of the heart whenever she detected signs of weakness in any of the hardier vegetables. She was grateful for the toil in which she could dwell as a sort of refuge from deeper thought.

—MARTHA OSTENSO

Adam was a gardener, and God, who made him, sees that half of all good gardening is done upon the knees.

—RUDYARD KIPLING

Should a garden look as if the gardener worked on his knees? I ask you.

—LINCOLN STEFFENS

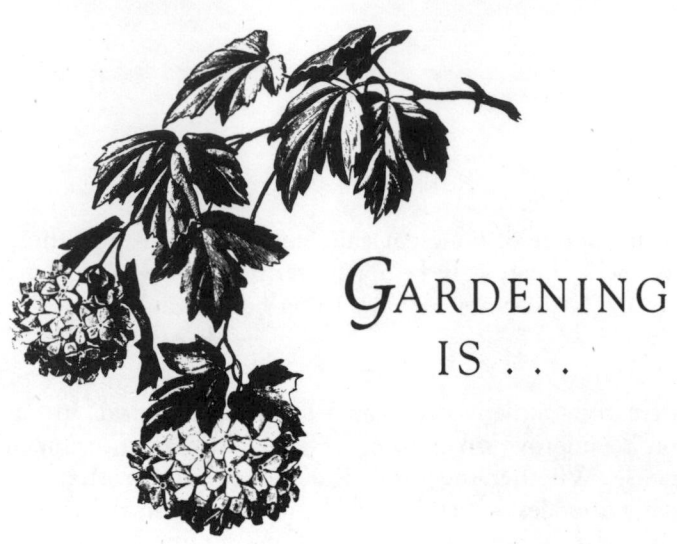

GARDENING IS . . .

*Gardening is a matter of your
enthusiasm holding up until your
back gets used to it.*

—ANONYMOUS

Planting is one of my great amusements, and even of those things which can only be for posterity, for a Septuagenary has no right to count on any thing beyond annuals.

—THOMAS JEFFERSON

To create a garden is to search for a better world. In our effort to improve on nature, we are guided by a vision of paradise. Whether the result is a horticultural masterpiece or only a modest vegetable patch, it is based on the expectation of a glorious future. This hope for the future is at the heart of all gardening.

—MARINA SCHINZ

Everything else about my garden was good and sometimes even thrilling, but this was what *gardening* was: The soft sound of the shovel thrusting into and dislodging the earth. Feeling the warmth of the sun on my shoulders. The earth against my knees. Savoring the undisturbed hours of solitary work.

—RICHARD GOODMAN

Gardening can become a kind of disease. It infects you; you cannot escape it. When you go visiting, your eyes rove about the garden; you interrupt the serious cocktail drinking because of an irresistible impulse to get up and pull a weed. —LEWIS GANNIT

Gardening has compensations out of all proportions to its goals. It is creation in the pure sense.
—PHYLLIS McGINLEY

Gardening is a craft, a science, and an art. To practice it well requires the enthusiasm of the true amateur and the understanding of the true student.
—LOUISE AND JAMES BUSH-BROWN

Gardening is an exercise in optimism. Sometimes, it is the triumph of hope over experience. —MARINA SCHINZ

Gardening is an instrument of grace. —MAY SARTON

Gardening is not a rational act. —MARGARET ATWOOD

Painting is closely related to gardening but closer still is poetry.
—ROBERT DASH

There can be no other occupation like gardening in which, if you were to creep up behind someone at their work, you would find them smiling.   —MIRABEL OSLER

Any fool can hope for splendour—
a simpleton may plant a seed.
We plant the fruit of God's provender,
matching foolish wish to deed.
                    —SIR KENNETH MERRICK

One for the rock, one for the crow,
One to die and one to grow.
                    —ENGLISH SAYING

The love of dirt is among the earliest of passions, as it is the latest.   —CHARLES DUDLEY WARNER

The love of gardening is a seed that once sown never dies.
                    —GERTRUDE JEKYLL

Give fools their gold, and knaves their power;
Let fortune's bubbles rise and fall;
Who sows a field, or trains a flower,
Or plants a tree, is more than all.
—JOHN GREENLEAF WHITTIER

I think this is what hooks one on gardening: it is the closest
one can come to being present at creation.
—PHYLLIS THEROUX

The trouble with gardening is that it does not remain an
avocation. It becomes an obsession. —PHYLLIS McGINLEY

Little by little, even with other cares, the slowly but surely
working poison of the garden-mania begins to stir in my
long-sluggish veins. —HENRY JAMES

One of the things that gardening does for you is to allow
you to bring into the world of exchange a wealth of cheap
biodegradable goods of unsurpassable quality. All but patho-
logically stingy gardeners are generous with whatever they
grow. This has nothing to do with wealth, which is early
schooled against the dangers of generosity. It has to do with
natural abundance, with the seeming ease with which
plants and trees bear, compared to the onerous labor re-
quired to craft anything by hand. —STANLEY CRAWFORD

Nothing is a better lesson in the knowledge of plants than to sit down in front of them, and handle them and look them over just as carefully as possible . . . and giving plenty of time to each kind of little plant, examining it closely and asking oneself, and it, why this and why that.

—GERTRUDE JEKYLL

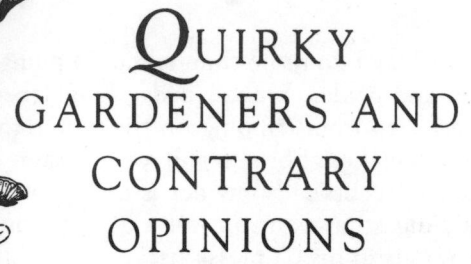

QUIRKY GARDENERS AND CONTRARY OPINIONS

I just come and talk to the plants, really—very important to talk to them, they respond I find.

—PRINCE CHARLES

Sometimes in May I do more than admire. I plunge into the sea of green and golden broom, dodge bumblebees seeking nectar, try to keep from tripping on the wisteria vines, and snip off a few branches of broom and some clusters of wisteria to bring home. Technically my act is theft, but I've always thought St. Augustine went on just a little too much about those stolen pears in his Confessions. —ALLEN LACY

I'd tiptoe out to the back to see whether I could catch Grandfather in one of his interminable conversations with his flowers.

—HELEN HAYES

A garden is like those pernicious machineries which catch a man's coat-skirt or his hand, and draw in his arm, his leg, and his whole body to irresistible destruction.

—RALPH WALDO EMERSON

The current fad for talking and singing to plants and telling them we love them will probably result in nothing more impressive than a vastly increased rate of plant mortality—as gardeners proceed farther and farther down the foolish road of what they presume to be utter communion.

—HENRY MITCHELL

I like to see flowers growing, but when they are gathered, they cease to please. I look on them as things rootless and perishable; their likeness to life makes me sad. I never offer flowers to those I love; I never wish to receive them from hands dear to me.   —CHARLOTTE BRONTË

A garden was the primitive prison, till man, with Promethean felicity and boldness, luckily sinned himself out of it.

—CHARLES LAMB

My father thought it unsuitable for a man to study flowers.

—RUPERT C. BARNEBY

No matter how skillfully carried out, I abhor the introduction of electricity into the garden. Lighted pools, false dawns among the shrubs are to me both ugly and vulgar. (No, I don't like *son et lumière* either: The Parthenon bathed in lavender is a horrid sight.) A path or driveway may need to be discreetly lighted to keep people from breaking their necks, and hurricane lamps on a terrace where one is dining are more than permissible. I love an old-fashioned Japanese paper lantern stuck with a candle and hung in a tree like a moon. A spotlight trained on a fountain, no. A garden at night should be itself—a place at rest, a haven for creatures, and for me too when I want to lie in the hammock in the dark.   —ELEANOR PERENYI

No one is ever at ease in a garden unless it looks like open country.   —JOHANN WOLFGANG VON GOETHE

The maples and ferns are still uncorrupt; yet no doubt, when they come to consciousness, they too will curse and swear.   —RALPH WALDO EMERSON

The more I hear of Horticulture, the more I like plain gardening.   —JULIAN R. MEADE

The more help a man has in his garden, the less it belongs to him.
—WILLIAM H. DAVIES

Today I was plowing faithfully through a horticultural tome when I came to a chapter which began thus, "If you would have a really successful garden, it behooves you . . ."

The hell it does. My garden is one place in the world where I am not behooved. —JULIAN R. MEADE

You could hardly see any beautiful, pale, bright, yellow-green of spring, every tree appeared to be entirely covered with a waving mass of pink or mauve tissue paper. The daffodils were so thick on the ground that they too obscured the green, they were new varieties of terrifying size, either dead white or dark yellow, thick and fleshy; they did not look at all like the fragile friends of one's childhood. The whole effect was of a scene for musical comedy.

—JESSICA MITFORD

Red geraniums were invented to show that even a flower could be hideous.   —WILLIAM MORRIS

Some people seem to forget that a plant is very like a human being. It is much nicer, of course, and much prettier and much pleasanter than a human being, but we are bound to admit the resemblance.   —BEVERLEY NICHOLS

We learned by trial and a great deal of error what could be grown there, and from studying books that recommended plants that would flourish in deep shade. So many of these were poisonous that we once contemplated going into business as market gardeners to supply would-be murderers who hesitated to sign chemists' registers for their needs.   —MAUREEN AND BRIDGET BOLAND

Democracy is fine in politics. It should stay there, and we need more of it. But its political virtue is no reason to practice it in the garden.   —ALLEN LACY

Exclusiveness in a garden is a mistake as great as it is in society.   —ALFRED AUSTIN

For it seems that proper gardeners never sit in their gardens. Dedicated and single-minded, the garden draws them into its embrace where their passions are never assuaged unless they are on their knees. But for us, the unserious, the improper people, who plant and drift, who prune and amble, we fritter away little dollops of time in sitting about our gardens. Benches for sunrise, seats for contemplation, resting perches for the pure sublimity of smelling the evening air or merely ruminating about a distant shrub. We are the unorthodox gardeners who don't feel compulsion to pull out campion among the delphiniums; we can idle away vacantly small chunks of time without fretting about an outcrop of buttercups groping at the pulsatillas. Freedom to loll goes with random gardening, it goes with the modicum of chaos which I long to see here and there in more gardens.   —MIRABEL OSLER

I would rather see one happy plant of knotweed than half a dozen aristocratic invalids struggling unsuccessfully.
                                                        —MARGUERITE JAMES

Sido loathed flowers to be sacrificed. Although her one idea was to give, I have seen her refuse a request for flowers to adorn a hearse or a grave. She would harden her heart, frown, and answer "No" with a vindictive look.
                                                        —COLETTE

The flower-arranger who is not a gardener should never be let loose with a knife or scissors out of doors, particularly near shrubs.   —MAUREEN AND BRIDGET BOLAND

Walter would not tolerate an unhealthy or badly grown plant and if he saw anything that wasn't looking happy he pulled it up. Often I would go out and find a row of sick looking plants laid out like a lot of dead rats.

—MARGERY FISH

A rose-tree stood near the entrance of the garden: the roses on it were white, but there were three gardeners at it, busily painting them red.   —LEWIS CARROLL

*A*UTUMN IN THE GARDEN

The scarlet of maples can shake me
  like a cry
Of bugles going by.
And my lonely spirit thrills
To see the frosty asters like smoke
upon the hills.

—WILLIAM BLISS CARMAN

Now Autumn's fire burns slowly along the woods.
—WILLIAM ALLINGHAM

Autumn is marching on: even the scarecrows are wearing dead leaves. —OTSUYU NAKAGAWA

October is nature's funeral month. Nature glories in death more than in life. The month of departure is more beautiful than the month of coming—October than May. Every green thing loves to die in bright colors.
—HENRY WARD BEECHER

Even if something is left undone, everyone must take time to sit still and watch the leaves turn.
—ELIZABETH LAWRENCE

Fall is not the end of the gardening year; it is the start of next year's growing season. The mulch you lay down will protect your perennial plants during the winter and feed the soil as it decays, while the cleaned-up flower bed will give you a huge head start on either planting seeds or setting out small plants. —THALASSA CRUSO

Heap high the farmer's wintry hoard!
    Heap high the golden corn!
No richer gift has Autumn poured
    From out her lavish horn!
        —JOHN GREENLEAF WHITTIER

I saw old Autumn in the misty morn
Stand shadowless like Silence, listening
To silence.
        —THOMAS HOOD

It was a morning of ground mist, yellow sunshine, and high rifts of blue, white-cloud-dappled sky. The leaves were still thick on the trees, but dew-spangled gossamer threads hung on the bushes and the shrill little cries of unrest of the swallows skimming the green open park spaces of the park told of autumn and change. —FLORA THOMPSON

It was Autumn, and incessant
    Piped the quails from shocks and sheaves,
And, like living coals, the apples
    Burned among the withering leaves.
        —HENRY WADSWORTH LONGFELLOW

153   Autumn in the Garden

O wild West Wind, thou breath of Autumn's being,
Thou, from whose unseen presence the leaves dead
Are driven, like ghosts from an enchanter fleeing.
—PERCY BYSSHE SHELLEY

Once more the weird laughter of the loons comes to my ear, the distance lends it a musical, melancholy sound. From a dangerous ledge off the lighthouse island floats in on the still air the gentle tolling of a warning bell as it swings on its rocking buoy; it might be tolling for the passing of summer and sweet weather with that persistent, pensive chime. —CELIA THAXTER

Just before the death of flowers,
And before they are buried in
snow,
There comes a festival season
When Nature is all aglow.
—ANONYMOUS

Pleasures lie thickest where no pleasures seem:
There's not a leaf that falls upon the ground
But holds some joy of silence or of sound,
Some spirits begotten of a summer dream.
—LAMAN BLANCHARD

The leaves fall early this autumn, in wind.
The paired butterflies are already yellow with August
Over the grass in the West garden.
—Ezra Pound

The melancholy days are come, the saddest of the year,
Of wailing winds, and naked woods, and meadows brown
and sear.   —W. C. Bryant

The stillness of October gold
Went out like beauty from a face.
—E. A. Robinson

Walked for half an hour in the garden. A fine rain was
falling, and the landscape was that of autumn. The sky was
hung with various shades of gray, and mists hovered about
the distant mountains—a melancholy nature. The leaves
were falling on all sides like the last illusions of youth under
the tears of irremediable grief. A brood of chattering birds

were chasing each other through the shrubberies, and playing games among the branches, like a knot of hiding schoolboys. Every landscape is, as it were, a state of the soul, and whoever penetrates into both is astonished to find how much likeness there is in each detail.

—HENRI FREDERIC AMIEL

I long for the bulbs to arrive, for the early autumn chores are melancholy, but the planting of bulbs is the work of hope and always thrilling.

—MAY SARTON

Every year, in November, at the season that follows the hour of the dead, the crowning and majestic hour of autumn, reverently I go to visit the chrysanthemums. . . . They are, indeed, the most universal, the most diverse of flowers.   —MAETERLINCK

The third day comes a frost, a killing frost.

—WILLIAM SHAKESPEARE

There comes a time when it cannot be put off any longer. The radio warns of a killing frost coming that night, and you must say good-by to the garden. You dread it, as you dread saying good-by to any good friend; but the garden waits with its last gifts, and you must go with a bushel basket or big buckets to receive them.   —RACHEL PEDEN

Now thin mists temper the slow-ripening beams
Of the September sun; his golden gleams
On gaudy flowers shine, that prank the rows
Of high-grown hollyhocks, and all tall shows
That Autumn flaunteth in his busy bowers;
Where tomtits, hanging from the drooping heads
Of giant sunflowers, peck the nutty seeds;
And in the feather aster bees on wing
Seize and set free the honied flowers,
Till thousand stars leap with their visiting:
While ever across the path mazily flit,
Unpiloted in the sun,
The dreamy butterflies
With dazzling colours powdered and soft glooms,
White, black and crimson stripes, and peacock eyes
Or on chance flowers sit,
With idle effort plundering one by one
The nectaries of deepest-throated blooms.
                              —ROBERT BRIDGES

September twenty-second, Sir, the bough cracks with un-
picked apples, and at dawn the small-mouth bass breaks
water, gorged with spawn.   —ROBERT LOWELL

Fresh October brings the pheasant,
Then to gather nuts is pleasant.
                    —SARA COLERIDGE

Listen! the wind is rising,
and the air is wild with leaves,
We have had our summer evenings,
now for October eves!
                    —HUMBERT WOLFE

O suns and skies and clouds of June,
And flowers of June together,
Ye cannot rival for one hour
October's bright blue weather.
                    —HELEN HUNT JACKSON

October inherits summer's hand-me-downs: the last of the
ironweed, its purple silken tatters turning brown, and the
tiny starry white asters tumbling untidily on the ground
like children rolling with laughter; stiff, drying black-eyed
Susans whose dark eyes gleamed from July's roadsides; cone-
flowers with deep yellow petals surrounding brown pincush-
ion centers from which bumblebees still are sipping honey.
The assignment of yellow is taken up now by thin-leafed
wild sunflowers and artichokes.   —RACHEL PEDEN

The sweet calm sunshine of October, now
    Warms the low spot; upon its grassy mold
The purple oak-leaf falls; the birchen bough
    Drops its bright spoil like arrow-heads of gold.
                                        —W. C. Bryant

I grow old, I grow old, the garden says. It is nearly October.
The bean leaves grow paler, now lime, now yellow, now
leprous, dissolving before my eyes. The pods curl and do
not grow, turn limp and blacken. The potato vines wither
and the tubers huddle underground in their rough weather-
proof jackets, waiting to be dug. The last tomatoes ripen
and split on the vine; it takes days for them to turn fully
now, and a few of the green ones are beginning to fall off.
                                        —Robert Finch

If it is true that one of the greatest pleasures of gardening
lies in looking forward, then the planning of next year's
beds and borders must be one of the most agreeable occupations in the gardener's calendar. This should make October
and November particularly pleasant months, for then we
may begin to clear our borders, to cut down those sodden
and untidy stalks, to dig up and increase our plants, and
to move them to other positions where they will show up
to greater effect. People who are not gardeners always say
that the bare beds of winter are uninteresting; gardeners
know better, and take even a certain pleasure in the neat-
ness of the newly dug, bare, brown earth.
                                        —Vita Sackville-West

Cornstalks from last summer's garden now lean toward the kitchen window, and the November wind goes through them in a shudder. Their thin tassels spread out beseeching fingers, and their long, bleached blades flutter like ragged clothing.
—RACHEL PEDEN

Dull November brings the blast,
Then the leaves are whirling fast.
—SARA COLERIDGE

❧ ❧ ❧

From the gardener's point of view, November can be the worst month to be faced: Nature is winding things down, the air is cold, skies are gray, but usually the final mark of punctuation to the year has yet to arrive—the snow; snow that covers all in the garden and marks a mind-set for the end of a year's activity. There is little to do outside except to wait for longer days in the new year and the joys of coming holidays. —PETER LOEWER

November always seemed to me the Norway of the year.
—EMILY DICKINSON

No warmth, no cheerfulness, no healthful ease,
No comfortable feel in any member—
No shade, no shine, no butterflies, no bees,
No fruits, no flowers, no leaves, no birds—
November!
—THOMAS HOOD

November's sky is chill and drear,
November's leaf is red and sear.
—SIR WALTER SCOTT

The gloomy month of November, when the people of England hang and drown themselves. —JOSEPH ADDISON

Along the side roads the bright gold of thin-leafed wild sunflowers gleams from its dust covering and attracts the eye as quickly as mention of easy money. Purple ironweed is diminishing in the pastures; thistles are down to their last silken tassels; goldenrod pours its heap of raw gold into the general fund.   —RACHEL PEDEN

There was something frantic in their blooming, as if they knew that frost was near and then the bitter cold. They'd lived through all the heat and noise and stench of summertime, and now each widely opened flower was like a triumphant cry, "We will, we will make seed before we die."
    —HARRIETTE ARNOW

ALL THOSE LOVELY VEGETABLES

It's difficult to think anything but pleasant thoughts while eating a homegrown tomato.

—LEWIS GRIZZARD

I think that no matter how old or infirm I may become, I will always plant a large garden in the spring. Who can resist the feelings of hope and joy that one gets from participating in nature's rebirth? I certainly can't. It is one of the most natural human instincts to want to make things grow, to nourish our own bodies and those of the ones we love. Such instincts are not satisfied by going to the supermarket and buying an uninspired plastic bag of vegetables. In fact, that is one of the quickest ways to squelch our natural impulses. But if you let the vegetables emerge, you will have not only the satisfaction of harvesting good things to eat but also the profound serenity that derives from a personal relationship with the earth.   —EDWARD GIOBBI

Cabbages, whose heads, tightly folded see and hear nothing of this world, dreaming only on the yellow and green magnificence that is hardening within them.   —JOHN HAINES

Most plants taste better when they've had to suffer a little.
—DIANA KENNEDY

Our vegetable garden is coming along well, with radishes and beans up, and we are less worried about revolution than we used to be. —E. B. WHITE

Ripe vegetables were magic to me. Unharvested, the garden bristled with possibility. I would quicken at the sight of a ripe tomato, sounding its redness from deep amidst the undifferentiated green. To lift a bean plant's hood of heart-shaped leaves and discover a clutch of long slender pods hanging underneath could make me catch my breath. Cradling the globe of a cantaloupe warmed in the sun, or pulling orange spears straight from his sandy soil—these were the keenest of pleasures, and even today in the garden they're accessible to me, dulled only slightly by familiarity. —MICHAEL POLLAN

Sowe Carrets in your Gardens, and humbly praise God for them, as for a singular and great blessing. —RICHARD GARDINER

The first gathering of the garden in May of salads, radishes and herbs made me feel like a mother about her baby—how could anything so beautiful be mine. And this emotion of wonder filled me for each vegetable as it was gathered every year. There is nothing that is comparable to it, as satisfactory or as thrilling, as gathering the vegetables one has grown. —ALICE B. TOKLAS

The smell of manure, of sun on foliage, of evaporating water, rose to my head; two steps farther, and I could look down into the vegetable garden enclosed within its tall pale of reeds—rich chocolate earth studded emerald green, frothed with the white of cauliflowers, jewelled with the purple globes of eggplant and the scarlet wealth of tomatoes.   —DORIS LESSING

Tomatoes and squash never fail to reach maturity. You can spray them with acid, beat them with sticks and burn them; they love it.   —S. J. PERELMAN

My father grew vegetables and fruits as other men paint pictures. From the day when the first seed catalogues were found in the post office along in February, he planned, devised, forecast. He had the vision of his garden first in his mind, perfect and true, and then he plied his brush with practised hand. Scarlet, crimson, and madder he brought to life in radishes, tomatoes, beets. His eye pleasured in the blue-green of cabbage and cauliflower; in the rich orange and yellow of carrot and pumpkin; in the rhythm of line found in a crookneck squash, and in the feminine grace of an ear of corn. So far as his own hand could govern, the canvas followed the vision, but he was ever at the mercy of the elements.   —DELLA T. LUTES

When autumn came, the last harvest was so occupying that one forgot that it meant leaving the garden for the return to Paris. Not only did the winter vegetables have to be gathered and placed to dry for a day before packing, but their roots and leaves had to be put on the compost with manure and leaves and packed down for winter. The day the huge baskets were packed was my proudest in all the year. The cold sun would shine on the orange-coloured carrots, the green, yellow and white pumpkins and squash, the purple eggplants and a few last red tomatoes. They made for me more poignant colour than any post-Impressionist picture. Merely to look at them made all the rest of the year's pleasure insignificant.—ALICE B. TOKLAS

In the night the cabbages catch at the moon, the leaves drip silver, the rows of cabbages are series of little silver waterfalls in the moon.   —CARL SANDBURG

Own a few acres, lad, and keep it unencumbered and you'll not want for some'at to eat. You can always grow a few cabbages.   —LOUIS L'AMOUR

If any citie or towne should be besieged with the enemy, what better provision for the greatest number of people can be than every garden be sufficiently planted with carrots?
—RICHARD GARDINER

In their native land day lilies are considered particularly delicious gourmet magic, and almost every part of the plant—the flowers, the peeled stems, and the freshly sprouted shoots—is eaten.   —THALASSA CRUSO

I must tell you that I have had a whole field of garlic planted for your benefit, so that when you come, we may be able to have plenty of your favourite dishes.   —BEATRICE D'ESTE

Let first the onion flourish there,
Rose among the roots, the maiden-fair
Wine scented and poetic soul
Of the capacious salad bowl.
—ROBERT LOUIS STEVENSON

An onion can make people cry, but there's no vegetable that can make them laugh.   —ANONYMOUS

Digging potatoes is always an adventure, somewhat akin to fishing. There is forever the possibility that the next cast— or the next thrust of the digging fork—will turn up a clunker.   —JEROME BELANGER

*A*s for rosemary, I let it run all over
my garden walls, not only because
my bees love it but because it is the
herb sacred to remembrance and to
friendship, whence a sprig of it hath
a dumb language.

—SIR THOMAS MORE

If I had to choose just one plant for the whole herb garden,
I should be content with basil.   —ELIZABETH DAVID

Mint I grow in abundance and in all its varieties. How
many there are, I might as well try to count the sparks
from Vulcan's furnace beneath Etna. —WALAFRID STRABO

"Tom, the bay leaf I'm putting in this *boeuf a la mode* was
plucked from a tree growing in the garden of Thomas Hardy's
birthplace," Catherine called from the kitchen. She did not
really expect an answer and indeed none came from Tom,
sitting hunched over his typewriter, so she went on, almost
to herself, "I wonder if it's *wrong* of me to use it for cooking?
Perhaps I ought to have pressed it in *Jude the Obscure*, or the
poems, that would have been more suitable."

—BARBARA PYM

When . . . I picked the first big, ripe, juicy tomato of the season, I was so proud of what I'd done that I refused to let anyone cut it up until I'd paraded it around the entire neighborhood so that everyone else could see.

—DUANE G. NEWCOMB

The abundance of everything around was so great, that . . . over-ripe fruit strewed the ground unheeded, while peas and beanstalks, still loaded, were blackening and yellowing in the sun; and vegetables running on all sides to waste.

—ANNE MARSH

MEANINGS, METAPHYSICS, AND MEMORIES

There is a garden in every childhood,
an enchanted place where colors
are brighter, the air softer, and the
morning more fragrant than ever again.

—ELIZABETH LAWRENCE

Every time I go into a garden where the man or woman who owns it has a passionate love of the earth and of growing things, I find that I have come home. In whatsoever land or clime or race, in whatsoever language, we speak a common tongue; the everlasting processes of earth bind us as one, stronger than Leagues or Covenants can ever bind. —MARION CRAN

Is the fancy too far brought, that this love for gardens is a reminiscence haunting the race of that remote time when but two persons existed—a gardener named Adam, and a gardener's wife called Eve? —ALEXANDER SMITH

Love of flowers and all things green and growing is with many women a passion so strong that it often seems to be a sort of primal instinct, coming down through generation after generation. —HELENA RUTHERFORD ELY

I feel really frightened when I sit down to paint a flower. —HOLMAN HUNT

As for garden photographers, how differently they see things. With what ease the camera seems to compose a picture of great beauty with its discriminating lens. The naked eye can't censor some ugly sight on the periphery of vision; the photographer takes the perfect shot and picks for us just what we need to see.　　—MIRABEL OSLER

*E*ach flower is a soul opening out to nature.

　　　　　　—GERALD DE NERVAL

How miraculous that growing on my own little plot of land are plants that can turn the dead soil into a hundred flavours as different as horseradish and thyme, smells ranging from stinkhorn to lavender.　　—JOHN SEYMOUR

I like gardening but I have a very modest garden. . . . I do a little, but not much, they just grow. It's a miracle, the way God meant it.　　　　　—ELLEN GOODMAN

In gardening, one's staunchest ally is the natural lust for life each plant has, that strong current which surges through everything that grows. —JEAN HERSHEY

Once a century, all of a certain kind of bamboo flower on the same day. Whether they are in Malaysia or in a greenhouse in Minnesota makes no difference, nor does the age or size of the plant. They flower. Some current of an inner language passes between them, through space and separation, in ways we cannot explain in our language. They are all, somehow, one plant, each with a share of communal knowledge. —LINDA HOGAN

The dew of the rouge-flower
When it is spilled
Is simply water.
—FUKUZOYO CHIYO

The famous learned man Archibius, which wrote unto Antiochus King of Syria, affirmeth that tempests shall not be harmful to plants, or fruits, if the speckled toade inclosed in a new earthen pot, be buried in the middle of the Garden or Field. Others there are, which hang the feathers of the Eagle or Seales skin, in the middle of the Garden, or at the four corners of the same. —THOMAS HYLL

The root of a forget-me-not caught the drop of water by the hair and sucked her in, that she might become a floweret, and twinkle as brightly as a blue star on the green firmament of earth. —FREDERICK WILHELM CAROVE

The violets in the mountains have broken the rocks.
—TENNESSEE WILLIAMS

There are fairies at the bottom of our garden!
—ROSE FYLEMAN

There's always something rough and tumble about planting—because with our clumsy implements we must reach from our atmospheric element down into another, down into the darkness of the soil. —STANLEY CRAWFORD

Two of life's mysteries—how does the ship get into the bottle, and how does the pear get into the bottle of pear *eau de vie?*

The first, I am told, is done by strings. The second is a gardener's trick. Once the pear blossom kerns into tiny fruit, select a likely one and push it carefully on its branch into a large bottle. Keep the bottle in place with forked sticks placed firmly in the ground. Stop up the end with tape or wax, to keep insects out. The bottle acts as greenhouse and the pear swells. When it is ripe, the bottle is cut from the tree. —JANE GRIGSON

Writing about propagation by cuttings:
Do you not realize that the whole thing is miraculous? It is exactly as though you were to cut off your wife's leg, stick it in the lawn, and be greeted on the following day by an entirely new woman, sprung from the leg, advancing across the lawn to meet you. Surely you would be surprised if, having snipped off your little finger, and pushed it into a flower pot, you were to find a miniature edition of yourself in the flower pot a day later? —BEVERLEY NICHOLS

Yet mark'd I where the bolt of Cupid fell:
It fell upon a little western flower,
Before milk-white, now purple with love's wound,
And maidens call it, Love-in-idleness.
Fetch me that flower; the herb I show'd thee once:
The juice of it on sleeping eyelids laid
Will make or man or woman madly dote
Upon the next live creature that it sees.
—WILLIAM SHAKESPEARE

On meeting Gertrude Jekyll:
We met at a tea-table, the silver kettle and the conversation reflecting rhododendrons. —SIR EDWIN LUTYENS

In a coign of the cliff between lowland and highland,
At the sea-down's edge between windward and lee,
Walled round with rocks as an inland island,
The ghost of a garden fronts the sea.
                    —ALGERNON CHARLES SWINBURNE

Some hang above the tombs,
Some weep in empty rooms,
I when the iris blooms,
    Remember.

I, when the cyclamen
Opens her buds again,
Rejoice a moment—then
    Remember.
                    —MARY COLERIDGE

There is something in all of us which responds to something we have known in our childhood. It may be a scent,
or a touch, or a sight, or anything which evokes a memory.

For some of us this evocation arises from the recollection of flowers we saw growing in our grandparents' gardens and now search for in vain.   —VITA SACKVILLE-WEST

The poppy is to me, like the Evening Primrose, a flower of mystery. Men have had many beautiful thoughts about it, and I have had mine. Its sunny face, like a cup filled with light, is as open as a child's heart, but its drooping, sleepy buds seems always to be holding back something. The Poppy fascinates me. It must be the hypnotist of the garden. Its seeds bring sleep.   —ABRAM LINWOOD URBAN

Someone said that God gave us memory so that we might have roses in December.   —SIR J. M. BARRIE

Flowers are Love's truest language.   —PARK BENJAMIN

Flowers are words
Which even a babe may understand.   —ARTHUR C. COXE

My garden is an honest place. Every tree and every vine are incapable of concealment, and tell after two or three months exactly what sort of treatment they have had. The sower may mistake and sow his peas crookedly: the peas make no mistake, but come up and show his line.
    —RALPH WALDO EMERSON

Flowers have an expression of countenance as much as men or animals. Some seem to smile, some have a sad expression, some are pensive and diffident, others again are plain, honest and upright. —HENRY WARD BEECHER

The daisy's for simplicity and unaffected air.
—ROBERT BURNS

The greatest delight the fields and woods minister is the suggestion of an occult relation between man and the vegetable. I am not alone and unacknowledged. They nod to me and I to them.
—RALPH WALDO EMERSON

The rose is the flower of Venus; and Love, in order that her sweet dishonesties might be hidden, dedicated this gift of his mother to Harpocrates, the god of silence. Hence the host hangs the rose over his friendly tables, that his guests may know that beneath it what is said will be regarded as a secret. —ANONYMOUS

There's rosemary, that's for remembrance . . . and there is pansies, that's for thoughts.   —WILLIAM SHAKESPEARE

To me the meanest flower that blows can give
Thoughts that do often lie too deep for tears.
                                        —WILLIAM WORDSWORTH

THE FRUIT GARDEN

A handsomely contrived, and well furnished Fruit Garden is an Epitome of Paradise, which was a most glorious place without a palace.

—JOHN EVELYN

ᔡ ᔡ ᔡ

If every boy in America planted an apple tree (except in
our compactest cities) in some useless corner, and tended
it carefully, the net saving would in no time extinguish the
public debt.　　　　　　　　　　　　—AMELIA SIMMONS

A little peace in an orchard grew—A little peach of emer-
　　ald hue;
Warmed by the sun and wet by the dew,
It grew.　　　　　　　　　　　　　　—EUGENE FIELD

In an orchard there should be enough to eat, enough to
lay up, enough to be stolen, and enough to rot upon the
ground.　　　　　　　　　　　　　—JAMES BOSWELL

In the corridors under there is nothing but sleep.
And stiller than ever an orchard boughs they keep
Tryst with the moon, and deep is the silence, deep
On moon-washed apples of wonder.
　　　　　　　　　　　　　　—JOHN DRINKWATER

It will beggar a doctor to live where orchards thrive.

—SPANISH PROVERB

The apple was the first fruit of the world, according to Genesis, but it was no Cox's orange pippin. God gave the crab apple and left the rest to man. This is perhaps what has made some suspect that the Tree of the Knowledge of Good and Evil was really a banana. After all, it was the earliest fruit taken into cultivation.   —JANE GRIGSON

What wondrous life is this I lead?
Ripe apples drop about my head;
The luscious clusters of the vine
Upon my mouth do crush their wine;
The nectarine and curious peach
Into my hands themselves do reach.

—ANDREW MARVELL

❧ ❧ ❧

Chestnuts in their spiky cases, sqashy medlars, and tart-tasting sorb apples—the autumn drives before it a profusion of modest fruits which one does not pick, but which fall into one's hands, which wait patiently at the foot of the tree until man deigns to collect them.   —COLETTE

When commerce was less efficient, I suspect that many more people grew pears. My husband remembers being taken by his mother to the Midlands before the First World War, and visiting house after house where pears were produced from back garden trees, as a special treat. They were sampled and compared as knowledgeably and thoughtfully as wine at a tasting.

—JANE GRIGSON

Strawberries, and only strawberries, could now be thought or spoken of. "The best fruit in England—everybody's favourite—always wholesome. These the finest beds and finest sorts. Delightful to gather for oneself—the only way of really enjoying them. Morning decidedly the best time—never tired—every sort good—hautboy infinitely superior—no comparison—the others hardly eatable—hautboys very scarce—Chili preferred—white wood finest flavour of all—price of strawberries in London . . . only objection to gathering strawberries the stooping—glaring sun—tired to death—could bear it no longer—must go and sit in the shade." Such, for half an hour, was the conversation.

—JANE AUSTEN

THERAPY IN THE GARDEN

Everybody needs beauty as well as bread, places to play in and pray in, where Nature may heal and cheer and give strength to body and soul alike.

—JOHN MUIR

Everything that slows us down and forces patience, everything that sets us back into the slow cycles of nature, is a help. Gardening is an instrument of grace. —MAY SARTON

Watching something grow is good for morale. It helps you believe in life. —MYRON S. KAUFMANN

Dead-heading the roses on a summer evening is an occupation to carry us back into a calmer age and a different century. Queen Victoria might still be on the throne. All is quiet in the garden; the paths are pale; our silent satellite steals up the sky; even the aeroplanes have gone to roost and our own nerves have ceased to twangle. There is no sound except the hoot of an owl, and the rhythmic snip-snap of our own secateurs, cutting the dead heads off, back to a new bud, to provoke new growth for the immediate future. —VITA SACKVILLE-WEST

Flowers . . . have a mysterious and subtle influence upon the feelings, not unlike some strains of music. They relax the tenseness of the mind. They dissolve its rigor.
—HENRY WARD BEECHER

Flowers and plants are silent presences; they nourish every sense except the ear. —MAY SARTON

I am weary of swords and courts and kings. Let us go into the garden and watch the minister's bees. —MARY JOHNSTON

In my garden I can find solitude. I can go out there and say, "No phones, no interruptions, I am busy," and then shut myself off for a little while. —HELEN HAYES

To dig in the mellow soil—to dig moderately, for all pleasures should be taken sparingly—is a great thing. One gets strength out of the ground as often as one really touches it with a hoe. . . . There is life in the ground; it goes into the seeds; and it also, when it is stirred up, goes into the person who stirs it. —CHARLES DUDLEY WARNER

Flowers always make people better, happier, and more helpful; they are sunshine, food and medicine to the soul.

—LUTHER BURBANK

Most gardeners I know would recoil from the suggestion that gardening is therapy, but they must know in their hearts that it helps that part of the brain or soul that this materialistic, competitive, noisy culture tends to unravel or destroy altogether. It is an antidote for the way many must earn their living. A garden must be the final refuge from progress and its relentless toll on "civilized" man.

—WILLIAM LONGGOOD

My good hoe as it bites the ground revenges my wrongs, and I have less lust to bite my enemies. In smoothing the rough hillocks, I smoothe my temper.

—RALPH WALDO EMERSON

Once we become interested in the progress of the plants in our care, their development becomes a part of the rhythm of our own lives and we are refreshed by it.

—THALASSA CRUSO

One of the healthiest ways to gamble is with a spade and a package of garden seeds.   —DAN BENNETT

There is one thing that you will find practically impossible to carry into your own greenhouse and that is tension.

—CHARLES H. POTTER

There's something soothing about firming seeds in the soil and tending plants under the glass of your greenhouse while raindrops and snowflakes fall against the panes.

—GEORGE ABRAHAM

When I was most tired, particularly after a hot safari in the dry, dusty plains, I always found relaxation and refreshment in my garden. It was my shop window of loveliness, and Nature changed it regularly that I might feast my hungry eyes upon it.

—OSA JOHNSON

CREATURES IN THE GARDEN

To me, the garden is a doorway to
other worlds; one of them, of course,
is the world of birds. The garden
is their dinner table, bursting with
bugs and worms and succulent berries
(so plant more to accomodate
you both).

—ANNE RAVER

A cow is a very good animal in the field; but we turn her out of a garden. —SAMUEL JOHNSON

Birds by day and skunk by night search for juicy grubs under damp mulch covering the potatoes. They hurl the thatch aside, unearthing the biggest and best spuds, it seems, and exposing them to sunlight that turns potatoes green, toxic, and fit only for compost. It is nip and tuck whether the sun or I will get to them first. Robins are especially vigorous in searching out the grubs. The garden feeds a large and varied clientele. —WILLIAM LONGGOOD

During the past few years there has been a wonderful resurgence around here of the many wild things with which man shares the living world. Nights have been brilliant with the flashes of fireflies, long absent in such quantities; there are unusual birds in every yard . . . and wherever you look, the flowers and hedgerows are alive with swarms of butterflies in flashing colors. I am delighted to see all this, but I am particularly happy with the return of the butter-flies, clouds of color which represent the reemergence of a

native that it was feared might have been lost forever through the overuse of powerful sprays.
—THALASSA CRUSO

I never suffer any of my family to kill those little innocent animals called striped snakes, for they do me much service in destroying grasshoppers and other troublesome insects. Toads are of essential service, especially in a garden, to eat up cabbage worms, caterpillars, etc. —FARMER'S ALMANAC

My tiger cat, taught only by nature, is a great believer in the efficacy of fragrant breathing and nibbling. For long intervals Orphie will sit in his favorite spot surrounded by catnip, thyme, burnet, and rue, swaying and rocking gently back and forth singing to himself—his eyes slowly closing—his nose high, sniffing, sniffing—this side, now that side—the collected fragrances of the garden. Orphie knows the virtues of my herbs. Occasionally he picks his way delicately among the plots nipping off a leaf here and a flower there, then stretches out on his favorite flagstone, the fragrant thyme all about him, and goes to sleep feeling that all's right in his world.   —ROSETTA E. CLARKSON

One morning I met the neighbouring cats who were prowling round looking for nests and listening for the cheeps of the tender young birds. They were threatened with my hosepipe and I hope they will now cease to prowl for a few days.   —ROSEMARY VEREY

I do not hesitate to interfere with nature on many occasions. I chase off cats trying to catch infant squirrels, and I frequently dip drowning bugs out of the fish pool. The mere fact that it is natural for cats to catch squirrels makes no difference to me; it is also natural for me to chuck rocks at the damned cats. Nature does not hesitate to interfere with me, so I do not hesitate to tamper with it.

—HENRY MITCHELL

Poor indeed is the garden in which birds find no homes.

—ABRAM LINWOOD URBAN

Somewhere among the rocks in the pond lives a small tortoise—left in the garden, probably, by the previous tenants of the house. It is very pretty, but manages to remain invisible for weeks at a time. In popular mythology, the tortoise is the servant of the divinity Kompira; and if a pious fisherman finds a tortoise, he writes upon his back characters signifying "Servant of the Deity Kompira," and then gives it a drink of sake and sets it free. It is supposed to be very fond of sake.

—LAFCADIO HEARN

The bees have given me a terrible fright this spring. They live in our roof and have done as long as I can remember. We rely on them for fertilising the fruit blossom and for many other services around the garden, including just being there to watch and enjoy. They make their first sortie on a sunny day in February to gather pollen from the willow catkins and wide-open crocuses, and from then on I see them around on sunny days. This year there was no sign of them, either working in the garden or going in and out of the roof. I value them so highly that I was beginning to make plans to get a hive ready for another swarm; but this would not have been quite the same; the roof dwelling bees are old friends. I could hardly believe my eyes a few days later when I looked up and there, silhouetted against the sky, was a crowd of bees flying lazily around, going slowly in and out of the roof tiles as if they had only just woken. What could they have been doing these last three months?

—ROSEMARY VEREY

The world has different owners at sunrise.... Even your own garden does not belong to you. Rabbits and blackbirds have the lawns; a tortoise-shell cat who never appears in daytime patrols the brick walls, and a golden-tailed pheasant glints his way through the iris spears.

—ANNE MORROW LINDBERGH

To the broad coping stone of the wall under the lime-boughs speckled thrushes came almost hourly to peer out and reconnoitre if it was safe to visit the garden, sometimes to see if a snail had climbed up the ivy. They then dropped quietly down into the long strawberry patch immediately under. The cover of strawberries is the constant recourse of all creeping things; the thrushes looked round every plant and under every leaf and runner. One toad always resided there, often two, and as you gathered a ripe straw-berry you might catch sight of his black eye watching you take the fruit he had saved for you.   —RICHARD JEFFRIES

Toads are conservative animals, I think, and not much given to expecting the best from fortune. Some weeks ago, well before the end of October, I accidentally dug up one while turning over some garden earth. I was surprised, naturally, when one of the clods heaved over on its side and there, in some annoyance, sat a toad. —HENRY MITCHELL

We have descended into the garden and caught three hundred slugs. How I love the mixture of the beautiful and the squalid in gardening. It makes it so lifelike.
—EVELYN UNDERHILL

Wonderful spiders' webs have been festooning our garden recently. On misty mornings each gossamer thread has a spangle of moisture to outline its pattern. This morning they were almost the best I had ever seen. One thread was slung across a path to alight on top of a juniper. There was a perfect symmetrical web but the thread went on to the next plant, a grindelia given me several years ago by Tony Venison. Here each stem end had a veil of web over it and so, miraculously, it went on. To see the spider in action it is best to go out at night with a torch. The spider is carnivorous and gets rid of many of our garden pests for us. Most garden spiders probably remake their webs every day. I wonder if there is a connection between this proliferation of webs and the plagues of flies that infest old houses on sunny October days? —ROSEMARY VEREY

You may go into the field or down the lane, but don't go into Mr. McGregor's garden. —BEATRIX POTTER

Birds are tyrants. They have a tyrannous effect on gardeners. We long to have them with us, but to hear their polyphony of song at four on a summer morning is something so dominant that it's hard to turn over and go back to sleep. Outside the garden is fermenting; it's so early, there are no shadows yet, there's almost a bloom lying over the garden; dew glistens on leaves and the smell of fresh petals percolates the bedroom. That urgency outside is not always possible to resist.   —MIRABEL OSLER

I hope you love birds, too. It is economical. It saves going to Heaven.
                                    —EMILY DICKINSON

I value my garden more for being full of blackbirds than of cherries, and very frankly give them fruit for their songs.
                                    —JOSEPH ADDISON

Many amateurs still think that when birds sing and hop around, they are being merry and affectionate. They are not, of course; they are being aggressive and demanding the price of a cup of coffee. As, however, human beings are soft at heart and in the head, I suppose we shall go on regarding this thing as a much loved garden bird, even when it beats on the window with its beak and tells you to get that goddam food out on the bird table or else.

—MILES KINGTON

I sincerely congratulate you on the arrival of the mockingbird. Learn all the children to venerate it as a superior being in the form of a bird, or as a being which will haunt them if any harm is done to itself or its eggs.

—THOMAS JEFFERSON

Shoot all the bluejays you want, if you can hit 'em, but remember it's a sin to kill a mockingbird. . . . Mockingbirds don't do one thing but make music for us to enjoy. They don't eat up people's gardens, don't nest in corncribs, they don't do one thing but sing their hearts out for us. That's why it's a sin to kill a mockingbird.   —HARPER LEE

The cuckoo comes in April,
Sings a song in May;
Then in June another tune,
And then she flies away.
                                    —ENGLISH RHYME

Today I am sure no one needs to be told that the more birds a yard can support, the fewer insects there will be to trouble the gardener the following year.

—THALASSA CRUSO

I continue to handpick the beetles, mosquitoes feast on me, birds eat the mosquitoes, something else eats the birds, and so on up and down the biotic pyramid.

—WILLIAM LONGGOOD

What if you do have a few bugs? A few bugs won't hurt you. Pick them off and drop them in a jar of water with a film of kerosene over it. Or let some of them eat up a few plants—the ones they choose will be weaklings, anyway, which you would pull out later. Unless you have a great big farm operation you won't get a huge invasion such as those that sometimes come to large fields of a single crop where the feasting is all too favorable.

—CATHARINE OSGOOD FOSTER

O cricket from your cheery cry
No one would ever guess
How quickly you must die.

—BASHO

I do believe that an intimacy with the world of crickets and their kind can be salutary—not for what they are likely to teach us about ourselves but because they remind us, if we will let them, that there are other voices, other rhythms, other strivings and fulfillments than ours.

       —DR. HOWARD ENSIGN EVANS

O'er folded blooms
 On swirls of musk,
The beetle booms adown the glooms
 And bumps along the dusk.
     —JAMES WHITCOMB RILEY

The ant finds kingdoms in a foot of ground.
     —STEPHEN VINCENT BENET

The first stop of my morning inspection tour is the spider who lives in the cucumber cage. His web is in the center, among the climbing vines, supported by long, stout silken threads like guy wires. The web would be almost invisible among the leaves were it not for pinpoints of dew that glisten in the morning sun. I have to be careful when gathering cucumbers not to disturb the spider or damage his web.   —WILLIAM LONGGOOD

We had a raccoon who left dusty paw prints all over a newly painted wooden gate, and another one that came and destroyed a white water lily imported from Africa, after which we set a trap, but we only caught a neighbor's cat. He was greatly put out when released but has continued to come back all the same, and through some unknown good fortune the coons have not.   —HENRY MITCHELL

Unexpected allies rally to my aid this morning. Tiny black ants crawl all over the potato plants attacking the grubs of potato beetles that I missed during yesterday's massacre. It is a grisly sight, this balancing of nature, although favorable to me. Ants by the thousands virtually cover the juicy, reddish-black humpback beetle grubs that squirt so revoltingly when pinched.   —WILLIAM LONGGOOD

Earth is a Garden

Apprentice yourself to nature. Not a
day will pass without her opening a new
and wondrous world of experience
to learn from and enjoy.

—Richard W. Langer

What would the world be once bereft
Of wet and wildness? Let them be left,
O let them be left, wildness and wet;
Long live the weeds and wilderness yet.
—GERARD MANLEY HOPKINS

The tints of autumn—a mighty flower garden blossoming
under the spell of the enchanter, Frost.
—JOHN GREENLEAF WHITTIER

Nature chose for a tool, not the earthquake or lightning to
rend and split asunder, not the stormy torrent or eroding
rain, but the tender snow-flowers noiselessly falling through
unnumbered centuries. . . .   —JOHN MUIR

Of al the floures in the mede,
Thanne love I most thise floures white and rede,
Swiche as men callen dayses in our toun.   —CHAUCER

Of the infinite variety of fruits which spring from the bosom of the earth, the trees of the wood are the greatest in dignity.　　　　　　　—SUSAN FENIMORE COOPER

I have always found thick woods a little intimidating, for they are so secret and enclosed. You may seem alone but you are not, for there are always eyes watching you. All the wildlife of the woods, the insects, birds, and animals, are well aware of your presence no matter how softly you may tread, and they follow your every move although you cannot see them.　　　　　　　—THALASSA CRUSO

That is the charm of woods, anyway. Things live and breathe quietly and out of sight. You can sense it, but you don't know what or even if it isn't the wood itself, more alive than it seems.　　　　　　　—L. M. BOSTON

Woodman, spare that tree!
Touch not a single bough!
In youth it sheltered me,
And I'll protect it now.
　　　—GENERAL GEORGE POPE MORRIS

Those green-robed senators of mighty woods,
Tall oaks, branch-charmed by the earnest stars,
Dream, and so dream all night without a stir.
—JOHN KEATS

Consider the lilies of the field, how they grow; they toil
not, neither do they spin: And yet I say unto you, That
even Solomon in all his glory was not arrayed like one of
these.   —NEW TESTAMENT

Global warming, ozone depletion, deforestation and over-
population are the four horsemen of a looming twenty-first
century apocalypse.   —MICHAEL OPPENHEIMER

*Hurt not the earth, neither the sea,
nor the trees.*
—THE BOOK OF REVELATION

I found a strawberry blossom in a rock. I uprooted it rashly
and felt as if I had been committing an outrage, so I planted
it again.   —DOROTHY WORDSWORTH

It is interesting to contemplate an entangled bank, clothed with many plants of many kinds, with birds singing on the bushes, with various insects flitting about, and with worms crawling through the damp earth, and to reflect that these elaborately constructed forms, so different from each other, and dependent on each other in so complex a manner, have all been produced by laws acting around us.

—CHARLES DARWIN

People have got to understand that the commandment, "Do unto others as you would that they should do unto you" applies to animals, plants and things, as well as to people! and that if it is regarded as applying only to people . . . then the animals, plants and things will, in one way or another, do as badly by man as man has done by them.

—ALDOUS HUXLEY

Remain true to the earth.   —FRIEDRICH NIETZSCHE

Short of Aphrodite, there is nothing lovelier on this planet than a flower, nor more essential than a plant. The true matrix of human life is the greensward covering mother earth. Without green plants we would neither breathe nor eat. On the undersurface of every leaf a million moveable lips are engaged in devouring carbon dioxide and expelling oxygen and food for man and beast.

—PETER TOMPKINS AND CHRISTOPHER BIRD

That sort of beauty which is called natural, as of vines, plants, trees, etc., consists of a very complicated harmony; and all the natural motions, and tendencies, and figures of bodies in the universe are done according to proportion, and therein is their beauty.   —JONATHAN EDWARDS

The plow is one of the most ancient and most valuable of man's inventions; but long before he existed the land was in fact regularly plowed, and still continues to be thus plowed by earthworms. It may be doubted whether there are many other animals which have played so important a part in the history of the world, as have these lowly organized creatures.   —CHARLES DARWIN

Touch the earth, love the earth, honour the earth, her plains, her valleys, her hills, and her seas; rest your spirit in her solitary places.
                    —HENRY BESTON

Earth laughs in flowers.   —RALPH WALDO EMERSON

In a rock garden we foster a little patch of the wilderness
that stands to us for freedom.   —JASON HILL

> Boon nature scattered, free and wild,
> Each plant or flower, the mountain's child.
>   —SIR WALTER SCOTT

But I was surprised when Wordsworth's Celandine appeared
in my garden, though I did not then, nor for several years
afterwards, know it for what it was. It was on an April
morning some eight years ago that I first came upon it, a
little spread of dark, heart-shaped leaves all decked out in
highly varnished yellow stars on a roughish piece of grow-
as-you-please bank that skirts the east side of my acre. It
was one of those surprises, perhaps undeserved, that come
to those who do not too anxiously order their gardens.
          —LOUISE BEEBE WILDER

I have often looked upon it as a piece of happiness that I
have never fallen into any of these fantastical tastes, nor
esteemed anything the more for its being uncommon and
hard to be met with. For this reason I look upon the whole
country in Springtime as a spacious garden, and make as
many visits to a spot of daisies, or a bank of violets, as a
florist to his borders or parterres.   —JOSEPH ADDISON

I know a bank whereon the wild thyme blows,
Where oxslips and the nodding violet grows,
Quite over-canopied with luscious woodbine,
With sweet musk-roses, and with eglantine.
—WILLIAM SHAKESPEARE

I saw the sweetest flower wild nature yields,
A fresh blown musk-Rose 'twas the first that threw
Its sweet upon the summer; graceful it grew
As in the wand that Queen Titania wields
And, as I feasted on its fragrance,
I thought the garden rose it much excelled.
—JOHN KEATS

O, see a world in a grain of sand,
And heaven in a wild flower.

—WILLIAM BLAKE

The Celandine:
Careless of thy neighborhood,
Thou dost show thy pleasant face
On the moor, and in the wood,
In the lane;—there's not a place,
Howsoever mean it be,
But 'tis good enough for thee.

—WILLIAM WORDSWORTH

Why are wildflowers so important to those of us who care at all for flowers? For me, anyway, it is because they come like gifts from God (or Nature), and to encounter them in their natural habitat is an extraordinary aesthetic pleasure.

—KATHARINE S. WHITE

Dandelions meet me wherever I am they overrun Germany's railway embankments dusty corners fields seize even well-trimmed gardens through hedges leaves like fine saws new flowers every day have the wind to carry them over rivers walled boundaries stick my fingers together when I try to fend them off.　　　　　—SARAH KIRSCH

When daises pied and violets blue
And lady-smocks all silver-white
And cuckoo-buds of yellow hue
Do paint the meadows with delight.
                    —WILLIAM SHAKESPEARE

A violet, by a mossy stone
    Half hidden from the eye!
Fair as a star, when only one
    Is shining in the sky.
                    —WORDSWORTH

WINTER IN THE GARDEN

In the bleak midwinter
Frosty wind made moan,
Earth stood hard as iron,
Water like a stone;
Snow had fallen, snow on snow,
Snow on snow,
In the bleak midwinter,
Long ago.

—CHRISTINA ROSSETTI

Winter is icummen in,
Lhude sing Goddamm.
Raineth drop and staineth slop,
And how the wind doth ramm!
Sing: Goddamm.
                    —EZRA POUND

When the gloom of dark December had quenched the summer's pride . . .   —CHARLOTTE BRONTË

The English winter, ending in July
To recommence in August.
                    —LORD BYRON

The most serious charge which can be brought against New
England is not Puritanism but February.
                    —JOSEPH WOOD KRUTCH

Late February days; and now at least,
Might you have thought that
Winter's Woe was past;
So fair the sky was and so soft the air.
                    —WILLIAM MORRIS

Probably more pests can be controlled in an armchair in front of a February fire with a garden notebook and a seed catalog than can ever be knocked out in hand-to-hand combat in the garden. —NEELY TURNER

The hiss was now becoming a roar—the whole world was a vast moving screen of snow—but even now it said peace, it said remoteness, it said cold, it said sleep.

—CONRAD AIKEN

The Snow-drop, Winter's timid child,
Awakes to life, bedew'd with tears.

—MARY ROBINSON

"Hurrah! blister my kidneys!" exclaimed he in delight, "it is a frost!—the dahlias are dead!" —R. S. SURTEES

All Nature seems at work. Slugs leave their lair—
The bees are stirring—birds are on the wing—
And Winter slumbering in the open air,
Wears on his smiling face a dream of spring!

—SAMUEL TAYLOR COLERIDGE

An important part in the winter landscape is played by the dead grasses and other herbaceous plants, especially by various members of the composite family, such as the asters, golden-rods, and sunflowers. Wreathed in snow or encased in ice, they present a singularly graceful and fantastic appearance. Or, perhaps, the slender stalks and branches armed with naked seed-pods trace intricate and delicate shadows on the smooth snow. —MRS. WILLIAM STARR DANA

Announced by all the trumpets of the sky,
Arrives the snow, and, driving o'er the fields,
Seems nowhere to alight: the withered air
Hides hills and woods, the river, and the heaven,
And veils the farm-house at the garden's end.
The sled and traveller stopped, the courier's feet
Delayed, all friends shut out, and housemates sit
Around the radiant fireplace, enclosed
In a tumultuous privacy of storm.
                              —RALPH WALDO EMERSON

Around the house flakes fly faster,
And all the berries are now gone
From holly and cotoneaster
Around the house. The flakes fly!—faster
Shutting indoors that crumb-outcaster
We used to see upon the lawn
Around the house. Flakes fly faster
And all the berries are now gone.
                              —THOMAS HARDY

For in spite of the snapdragons and the dusty millers and the cherry blossoms, it was always winter. —JANET FRAME

I prefer winter and fall, when you feel the bone structure in the landscape—the loneliness of it—the dead feeling of winter. Something waits beneath it—the whole story doesn't show. —ANDREW WYETH

> I wonder if the sap is stirring yet,
> If wintry birds are dreaming of a mate,
> If frozen snowdrops feel as yet the sun
> And crocus fires are kindling one by one:
>   Sing robin, sing;
> I still am sore in doubt concerning Spring.
>   CHRISTINA ROSSETTI

If we had no winter, the spring would not be so pleasant. —ANNE BRADSTREET

In the depths of winter I finally learned that within me there lay an invincible summer.

                    —ALBERT CAMUS

If Winter comes, can Spring be far behind?

—PERCY BYSSHE SHELLEY

Most people, early in November, take last looks at their gardens, and are then prepared to ignore them until the spring. I am quite sure that a garden doesn't like to be ignored like this. It doesn't like to be covered in dust sheets, as though it were an old room which you had shut up during the winter. Especially since a garden knows how gay and delightful it can be, even in the very frozen heart of the winter, if you only give it a chance.

—BEVERLEY NICHOLS

Soon will set in the fitful weather, with fierce gales and sullen skies and frosty air, and it will be time to tuck up safely my Roses and Lilies and the rest for their winter sleep beneath the snow, where I never forget them, but ever dream of their wakening in happy summers yet to be.

—CELIA THAXTER

That grand old poem called winter.

—HENRY DAVID THOREAU

The cold was our pride, the snow was our beauty. It fell and fell, lacing day and night together in a milky haze, making everything quieter as it fell, so that winter seemed to partake of religion in a way no other season did, hushed, solemn.

—PATRICIA HAMPL

The shortest day has passed, and whatever nastiness of weather we may look forward to in January and February, at least we notice that the days are getting longer. Minute by minute they lengthen out. It takes some weeks before we become aware of the change. It is imperceptible even as the growth of a child, as you watch it day by day, until the moment comes when with a start of delighted surprise we realize that we can stay out of doors in a twilight lasting for another quarter of a precious hour.

—VITA SACKVILLE-WEST

There is a privacy about it which no other season gives you. . . . In spring, summer and fall people sort of have an open season on each other; only in the winter, in the country, can you have longer, quiet stretches when you can *savor* belonging to yourself.   —RUTH STOUT

There seems to be so much more winter than we need this year.   —KATHLEEN NORRIS

When it's too cold for comfort, the sun-filled garden promises that winter will be brief.   —NORMAN KENT JOHNSON

When the ice of winter holds the house in its rigid grip, when curtains are drawn early against that vast frozen waste of landscape, almost like a hibernating hedgehog I relish the security of being withdrawn from all that summer ferment that is long since past. Then is the time for reappraisal: to spread out, limp and receptive, and let garden thoughts rise to the surface. They emerge from some deep source of stillness which the very fact of winter has released.   —MIRABEL OSLER

Winter is a time of promise because there is so little to do—or because you can now and then permit yourself the luxury of thinking so.   —STANLEY CRAWFORD

> I don't believe the half I hear,
> Nor the quarter of what I see!
> But I have one faith, sublime and true,
> That nothing can shake or slay;
> Each spring I firmly believe anew
> All the seed catalogues say!
>   -—CAROLYN WELLS

There are two seasonal diversions that can ease the bite of any winter. One is the January thaw. The other is the seed catalogues.   —HAL BORLAND

CHILDREN AND GARDENS

Gardening shouldn't be a grim business.
If you've forgotten that, it's time you
learned a lesson from your children.

—RICHARD NICHOLLS

The head-gardener was the terror of my life. He was an immensely dignified man, with a hooked nose, keen eyes, and a great black beard, giving him the appearance of a major prophet. From time to time he used to descend on me with accusations of having robbed his peach trees or destroyed his borders by picking flowers, accusations which were sometimes well founded and sometimes not. In those days I regarded him as an ogre and a spoil-sport, but looking back on him now I see that he was merely a typical head-gardener of the grander sort, justly exasperated by the depredations of an irresponsible child. Absolute lord in his own domain, he must have counted me among the worst of his garden pests. —VITA SACKVILLE-WEST

A clear memory of my own is of the time, when I was six years old, visiting the potting shed on my father's nursery and discovering a discarded box of seedlings of Gentiana verna which I seized and took to plant the seedlings in my own garden. Some months later I heard that the nursery had sold out all the gentian, and I was able to enter into business for the first time and sold them back to my father for a few pence each, a sum which was promptly expended on packets of seed. —WILL INGWERSEN

Mistress Mary worked in her garden until it was time to go to her midday dinner. In fact, she was rather late in remembering, and when she put on her coat and hat, and picked up her skipping-rope, she could not believe that she had been working two or three hours. She had been actually happy all the time; and dozens of the tiny, pale green points were to be seen in cleared places, looking twice as cheerful as they had looked before when the grass and weeds had been smothering them.

—FRANCES HODGSON BURNETT

I think of my flower beds as places to grow flowers. A good many kids think they make a fine shortcut to get to school. Apparently they see nothing wrong in stumbling over my chrysanthemums, liatris, and sedums when they're running late, meanwhile scattering candy wrapper and aluminum cola cans in their wake. —ALLEN LACY

I have read somewhere that no Japanese child will instinctively pick a flower, not even a very young child attracted by its bright color, because the sacredness of flowers is so deeply imbued in the culture of Japan that its children understand the blossoms are there to look at, not to pluck.

—KATHARINE S. WHITE

The neighbors' small children are also out of place in your garden, in strawberry and currant time. I hope I appreciate the value of children. We should soon come to nothing without them, though the Shakers have the best gardens in the world. Without them the common school would languish. But the problem is, what to do with them in a garden. For they are not good to eat, and there is a law against making away with them. The law is not very well enforced, it is true; for people do thin them out with constant dosing, paregoric, and soothing-syrups, and scanty clothing. But I, for one, feel that it would not be right, aside from the law, to take the life of even the smallest child, for the sake of a little fruit, more or less, in the garden. —CHARLES DUDLEY WARNER

To climb up, among the leaves, beyond the reach of intervention, must be the oldest, most joyous instinct in the world, the next best thing to flying. I can recall few keener pleasures and climbed trees until well past the age when it was decent to do so. . . .

To find a resting place about half way up, somewhere to stop and dream and read, or perhaps eat lunch, is an enjoyment no child should be denied—and I'm tempted to say, no adult either. When I spot a tree house on someone's property, I know civilized people live there, people whose idea of happiness goes beyond the provision of color TV. At the very least, they have made the gift of privacy and independence to a child, and if the child rejects those, he is past saving. —ELEANOR PERENYI

When I was a little girl, my mother took great pains to interest me in learning to know the birds and wild flowers and in planting a garden. I thought that roots and bulbs and seeds were as wonderful as flowers, and the Latin names on seed packages as full of enchantment as the counting-out rhymes that children chant in the spring. I remember the first time I planted seeds. My mother asked me if I knew the Parable of the Sower. I said I did not, and she took me into the house and read it to me. Once the relation between poetry and the soil is established in the mind, all growing things are endowed with more than material beauty.   —ELIZABETH LAWRENCE

Though I have only a tiny yard, I have given a place of honor to the grand Dutch crocuses, not only because I love them myself, but because I know few flowers are so attractive to children. I do not expect to see many flowers; I expect the children to pick them. For this reason I have planted them conveniently near the sidewalk. When children pick flowers, I do not like the word "steal," and the quickest possible route to hell, it has been said, is to growl at a child for picking crocuses. The child should be gently taught the curious customs of our society, that he should not pick flowers without permission, but it is intolerable to think of a child's excitement over these wonderful sweet gaudy flowers all ruined by harsh reproaches. Now of course if the child gets into Lilium langkongense or the irises, well, that is something else again, and a tub of boiling oil is recommended.   —HENRY MITCHELL

Off she ran with her little basket, but by the time she reached the plot of rough grass where the hamlet children played their country games it was too late; the sun had set, and the daisies were all asleep. There were thousands and thousands of them, but all screwed up, like tightly shut eyes. Laura was so disappointed that she sat down in the midst of them and cried. Only a few tears and very soon dried, then she began to look about her. The long grass in which she sat was a little wet, perhaps with dew, or perhaps with an April shower, and the pink-tipped daisy buds were a little wet, too, like eyes that had gone to sleep crying. The sky, where the sun had set, was all pink and purple and primrose. There was no one in sight and no sound but the birds singing and suddenly, Laura realized that it was nice to be there, out of doors by herself, deep in the long grass, with the birds and the sleeping daisies.

—FLORA THOMPSON

The trick is simple, but it requires concentration. Pinch off the green receptacle and ovary at the base of the long, trumpet-shaped flower, grasp the bottom of the pistil firmly between thumb and forefinger, and slowly pull it down through the tubular blossom until it emerges with a tiny, glistening drop of clear nectar to sip. And then another blossom, and another, each giving its perfume to the tip of the tongue. A child with a sufficient store of fresh honey-suckle blossoms becomes kin to the gods who feed on ambrosia, kin to the bee, the hummingbird, the lunar moth, to all the creatures of the air who pay their visits to this sweetest of all "serious weeds."   —ALLEN LACY

The pure happiness of picking water lilies on a New Hampshire lake. The lake was Chocorua, and picking water lilies was not an unusual event for my next-older sister and me. We spent the best summers of our girlhood on, or in, this lake, and we picked the lilies in the early morning, paddling to the head of the lake, where the water was calm at the foot of the mountain and the sun had just begun to open the white stars of the lilies. The stern paddle had to know precisely how to approach a lily, stem first, getting near enough so the girl in the bow could plunge her arm straight down into the cool water and break off the rubbery stem, at least a foot under the surface, without leaning too far overboard. It took judgement to select the three or four freshest flowers and the shapeliest lily pad to go with them, and it took skill not to upset the canoe. Once the dripping blossoms were gathered and placed in the shade of the bow seat, we paddled home while their heavenly fragrance mounted all around us. I know now that their lovely Latin name was Nymphaea odorata, but at the time I knew only that they were the common pond lily of northeast America.
     —KATHARINE S. WHITE

Our child must have been almost three on that breezy day in Berlin (where, of course, no one could escape familiarity with the ubiquitous picture of the Führer) when we stood, he and I, before a bed of pallid pansies, each of their upturned faces showing a dark mustache-like smudge, and had great fun, at my rather silly prompting, commenting on their resemblance to a crowd of bobbing little Hitlers.

—VLADIMIR NABOKOV

I don't know why but I somehow managed to let nasturtiums slip from consciousness, like old friends long neglected. And nasturtiums and I go very far back indeed. They were the first seeds my mother let me plant, when I was no more than five years old. Her choice was excellent. The seeds are large, about the size of an English pea, but corky and wrinkled. Children know for certain that they are planting something, with none of the doubt that might accompany the planting of petunias or nicotiana seeds, which look like fine brown dust.   —ALLEN LACY

GRASS

And wind moving through the grass
so that the grass quivers. This
moves me with an emotion I don't
even understand.

—KATHERINE MANSFIELD

A child said *What is the grass?* fetching it to one with full
    hands.
How could I answer the child? I don't know what it is any
    more than he.   —WALT WHITMAN

All flesh is grass.   —ISAIAH

Consider the many special delights a lawn affords: soft mat-
tress for a creeping baby; worm hatchery for a robin; cro-
quet or badminton court; baseball diamond; restful green
perspectives leading the eye to a background of flower border, shrubs, or hedge; green shadows . . . as changing and
as spellbinding as the waves of the sea, whether flecked
with sunlight under trees of light foliage, like elm and lo-
cust, or deep, dark, solid shade, moving slowly as the tide,
under maple and oak.   —KATHARINE S. WHITE

God said, Let the earth bring forth grass.   —GENESIS

Grass is hard and lumpy and damp, and full of dreadful
black insects.   —OSCAR WILDE

Grass is the forgiveness of nature—her constant benediction. . . . Forests decay, harvests perish, flowers vanish, but grass is immortal. —JOHN J. INGALLS

Grass is the forgiveness of nature. —THOMAS CARLYLE

Grass is the hair of the earth. —THOMAS DEKKER

Grass walks are only for those hours of the day when there is no dew, otherwise you must provide shoes or boots of extraordinary goodnesse. —GERVASE MARKHAM

Home would not be home without a lawn. —KATHARINE S. WHITE

How ow lush and lusty the grass looks! how green!
—WILLIAM SHAKESPEARE

❧ ❧ ❧

I believe a leaf of grass is no less than the journey-work of the stars. —WALT WHITMAN

Nothing is more pleasant to the Eye
than greene Grasse kept finely shorn.
—FRANCIS BACON

The lawn holds great appeal, especially to Americans. It looks sort of natural—it's green; it grows—but in fact it represents a subjugation of the forest as utter and complete as a parking lot. Every species is forcibly excluded from the landscape but one, and this is forbidden to grow longer than the owner's little finger. A lawn is nature under totalitarian rule.
—MICHAEL POLLAN

The murmur that springs
From the growing of grass.
—EDGAR ALLAN POE

The sight of a dandelion in bloom in the grass so inflamed [my father] that one bad year for dandelions he equipped his two younger daughters with jackknives and offered us ten cents a hundred dandelion roots, provided we cut them nice and deep.
—KATHARINE S. WHITE

There are no lawns in Chinese gardens: grass carries unpleasant images of cows or of invading hordes from the Mongolian steppes. Instead, there is paving, from large flagstones to intricate mosaics, like flowered carpets or with cheerful representations of lucky bats, or cranes, or turtles, or those most real and powerful entities, dragons.

—NANCY-MARY GOODALL

There is not a sprig of grass that shoots uninteresting to me.

—THOMAS JEFFERSON

What we loved best about England was the grass—the short, clean, incredibly green grass with its underlying tough, springy turf, three hundred years growing.

—HAN SUYIN

Whether we look, or whether we listen
We hear life murmur, or see it glisten;
Every clod feels a stir of might,
   An instinct within it that reaches and towers,
And, groping blindly above it for light,
   Climbs to a soul in grass and flowers.

—JAMES RUSSELL LOWELL

Grass grows at last above all graves.

—JULIA DORR

I bequeath myself to the dirt to grow from the grass I love,
If you want me again look for me under your boot-soles.
—WALT WHITMAN

Pile the bodies high at Austerlitz and Waterloo.
Shovel them under and let me work—
I am the grass; I cover all.
—CARL SANDBURG

CHANGING SEASONS

To everything there is a season,
and a time to every purpose under heaven.

—ECCLESIASTES

❧ ❧ ❧

"We're walking along in the changing-time," said Doc. "Any day now the change will come. It's going to turn from hot to cold. . . . Old Jack Frost will be pinching things up. Old Mr. Winter will be standing in the door. Hickory tree there will be yellow. Sweet-gum red, hickory yellow, dogwood red, sycamore yellow . . . persimmons will all get fit to eat, and the nut will be dropping like rain all through the woods here. And run, little quail, run, for we'll be after you too."
—EUDORA WELTY

January grey is here,
Like a sexton by her grave;
February bears the bier,
March with grief doth howl and rave,
And April weeps—but O ye hours!
Follow with May's fairest flowers.
—PERCY BYSSHE SHELLEY

Leaves are verbs that conjugate the seasons.
—GRETEL EHRLICH

Live in each season as it passes;
breathe the air, drink the drink,
taste the fruit, and resign yourself to
the influences of each.
— HENRY DAVID THOREAU

Sing a song of seasons;
 Something bright in all;
Flowers in the Summer;
 Fires in the Fall.
— ROBERT LOUIS STEVENSON

Snowy, Flowy, Blowy,
Showery, Flowery, Bowery,
Hoppy, Croppy, Droppy,
Breezy, Sneezy, Freezy.
— GEORGE ELLIS

Spring is a virgin, Summer a mother, Autumn a widow, and Winter a stepmother.   — POLISH PROVERB

Spring always seems to me like a courtship, summer like a marriage, autumn like a really grand party, and winter like a death, and yet a death that has in it an infinity of life.
— BEVERLEY NICHOLS

You mustn't rely on flowers to make your garden attractive. A good bone structure must come first, with an intelligent use of evergreen plants so that the garden is always clothed, no matter what time of year. Flowers are an added delight, but a good garden is the garden you enjoy looking at even in the depths of winter. —MARGERY FISH

To see a hillside white with dogwood bloom is to know a particular ecstasy of beauty, but to walk the gray Winter woods and find the buds which will resurrect that beauty in another May is to partake of continuity.

—HAL BORLAND

The way it works is this: summer is hot and winter is cold and the other seasons fall in between. Gardeners who every year go off the deep end at the first slight variation in mean temperature should try to get that sentence fixed in their heads. —HENRY MITCHELL

LESSONS FROM THE GARDEN

*There is no other door to knowledge
than the door Nature opens; and
there is no truth except the truths we
discover in Nature.*

—LUTHER BURBANK

"Book learning" gave me information, but only physical contact can give any real knowledge and understanding of a live organism. To have "green fingers" or a "green thumb" is an old expression which describes the art of communicating the subtle energies of love to prosper a living plant. . . . If you wish to make anything grow you must understand it, and understand it in a very real sense. "Green fingers" are a fact, and a mystery only to the unpractised. But green fingers are the extensions of a verdant heart. A good garden cannot be made by somebody who has not developed the capacity to know and to love growing things.　　　　　　　　　　　　　　—RUSSELL PAGE

A Garden should always look bigger than it really is.
　　　　　　　　　　　　　　—ALEXANDER LE BLOND

You can't be suspicious of a tree, or accuse a bird or a squirrel of subversion or challenge the ideology of a violet.
　　　　　　　　　　　　　　—HAL BORLAND

Command large fields, but cultivate small ones.　—VIRGIL

I feel every garden should have some element of mystery in its design: whatever the size, it is best if not all visible at once. The largest garden looks smaller if you can see it in one glance. Even in the smallest area it must be possible to plant so that there is some element of surprise: peer behind a shrub or over a low wall to discover some pleasant composition of textured leaves or a plant flowering secretly; turn a corner to be "surprised" by some new color; have your mood changed by stepping out of shadow into sunshine. Gardens should invite exploration with a path that curves out of sight: it may lead nowhere, but has the effect of making you feel that more is to come.

—PENELOPE HOBHOUSE

With a garden there is hope.
—GRACE FIRTH

Any one seed may be too old to sprout or inferior in some way, but it will never try to be something it isn't fitted to be. A man may study to be a surgeon when he should have been a shoemaker, a talented painter may spend his life trying to convince himself and his fellows that he is a lawyer, but a turnip seed will never attempt to grow into an ear of corn. If you plant a good turnip seed properly a turnip is what you will get every single time.

—RUTH STOUT

Firmness in all aspects is a most important quality when gardening, not only in planting but in pruning, dividing and tying up. Plants are like babies, they know when an amateur is handling them.   —MARGERY FISH

Good huswifes in summer will save their own seedes,
Against the next years, as occasions needes.
One seed for another, to make an exchange,
With fellowlie neighborhood seemeth not strange.
    —THOMAS TUSSER

Laws of Gardening:
  1. Other people's tools work only in other people's gardens.
  2. Fancy gismos don't work.
  3. If nobody uses it, there's a reason.
  4. You get the most of what you need the least.
    —ARTHUR BLOCH

This rule in gardening never forget:
To sow dry and to set wet.
    —ENGLISH PROVERB

On making mistakes in the garden:
That's how a gardener learns. It's not like making a mistake with the baby that the psychotherapist will trace back directly to you 20 years later. Plants don't point a finger. If they live, they don't carry grudges. If they die, unless you've

killed an entire species or a rain forest, you feel only momentary guilt, which is quickly replaced by a philosophical, smug feeling: Failure is enriching your compost pile.

—ANNE RAVER

Overfertilized plants may be beautiful but are otherwise useless, like people whose energies are devoted so completely to their appearance that there is no other development.

—WILLIAM LONGGOOD

A garden is a grand teacher. It teaches patience and careful watchfulness; it teaches industry and thrift; above all, it teaches entire trust.

—GERTRUDE JEKYLL

A modest garden contains, for those who know how to look and to wait, more instruction than a library.

—HENRI FREDERIC AMIEL

But a garden is at once the most delightful and cunning of teachers. How kindly are the virtues it inculcates!— Patience, faith, hope, tenderness, gratitude, resignation, things in themselves as fragrant and beautiful as the flowers, or like the herbs, a little repellent of aspect, but sweet in their bruised savor.

—AGNES AND EGERTON CASTLE

Gardening, I had by now come to appreciate, is a painstaking exploration of place; everything that happens in my garden—the thriving and dying of particular plants, the maraudings of various insects and other pests—teaches me to know this patch of land more intimately, its geology and microclimate, the particular ecology of its local weeds and animals and insects. My garden prospers to the extent I grasp these particularities and adapt to them.

—MICHAEL POLLAN

The more I prowl round my garden at this time of year, especially during that stolen hour of half-dusk between tea and supper, the more do I become convinced that a great secret of good gardening lies in covering every patch of the ground with some suitable carpeter. Much as I love the chocolate look of the earth in winter, when spring comes back I always feel that I have not done enough, not nearly enough, to plant up the odd corners with little low things that will crawl about, keeping weeds away, and tuck themselves into chinks that would otherwise be devoid of interest or prettiness.   —VITA SACKVILLE-WEST

Half the interest of a garden is in the constant exercise of the imagination.
—MRS. C. W. EARLE

I am the garden and every morn I am revealed in new beauty. Observe my dress attentively, and you will reap the benefit of a commentary on decoration.

—ANONYMOUS; APPEARS ON
A WALL OF THE ALHAMBRA IN SPAIN

I obstinately refused to accept the lore of the farmers, judging it, with the prejudice of a townswoman, to be nothing but superstition. They told me never to transplant parsley, and not to plant it on Good Friday. We did it in California, was my weak reply. They said not to plant at the moment of the new or full moon. The seed would be as indifferent as I was, was my impatient answer to this. But it was not. Before the end of our tenancy of the lovely house and gardens at Bilignin, I had become not only weather-wise but a fairly successful gardener.   —ALICE B. TOKLAS

I recommend that all bachelors have a garden. It will give them, in some small way, the experience of being a parent.
—RICHARD GOODMAN

In all places, then, and in all seasons,
Flowers expand their light and soul-like wings,
Teaching us by most persuasive reasons
How akin they are to human things.
—HENRY WADSWORTH LONGFELLOW

Most gardeners, I think, come to organic gardening through the kitchen door. Their first concern is fresh, uncontaminated vegetables, and it may seem less important to apply the same principles to trees, shrubs, lawns and flowers. But it doesn't make much sense to keep the kitchen garden free of poisons if you apply herbicides to the lawn and something that smells like boiled rubber to the flowers. A garden is a world, and its parts are not separable.

—ELEANOR PERENYI

The more one gardens, the more one learns; and the more one learns, the more one realizes how little one knows. I suppose the whole of life is like that: the endless complications, the endless difficulties, the endless fight against one thing or another, whether it be green-fly on the roses or the complexity of personal relationships.

—VITA SACKVILLE-WEST

There is material enough in a single flower for the ornament of a score of cathedrals.   —JOHN RUSKIN

There is no royal road. It is no use asking me or any one else how to dig—I mean sitting indoors and asking it. Better go and watch a man digging, and then take a spade and try to do it, and go on trying until it comes, and you gain the knack that is to be learnt with all tools, of the doubling of power and halving the effort; and meanwhile you will be learning other things, about your arms and legs and back ... and you will find out there are all sorts of ways of learning, not only from people and books, but from sheer trying. —GERTRUDE JEKYLL

To work in the garden is to be brought into contact with the elements of botany, geography, ecology, genetics, chemistry and entomology—not to mention ornithology, bacteriology and meteorology—and interest may develop in any of these directions. —ALICE M. COATS

When I am alone the flowers are really seen; I can pay attention to them. They are felt as presences. Without them I would die. Why do I say that? Partly because they change before my eyes. They live and die in a few days; they keep me closely in touch with process, with growth, and also with dying. I am floated on their moments.
—MAY SARTON

You eat and think differently when you have a garden. You have different expectations. One way and another, a garden is in your thoughts every day, what you are going to do in it or take from it. There is no ignoring it. A garden demands its share of time and attention; it helps shape the economy of our lives. —WILLIAM LONGGOOD

The love of flowers is really the best teacher of how to grow and understand them. —MAX SCHLING

WEATHER IN THE GARDEN

Weather means more when you have
a garden. There's nothing like
listening to a shower and thinking
how it is soaking in and around your
lettuce and green beans.

—MARCELENE COX

The North wind doth blow
And we shall have snow,
And what will the robin do then, poor thing?
　　　　—ANONYMOUS, NURSERY RHYME

A halo round the moon is a sign of wind.
　　　　—CHINESE PROVERB

A Summer fog for fair, a Winter fog for rain.
　　　　—ENGLISH PROVERB

Almighty and most merciful Father, we pray thee to send
us such seasonable weather that the earth may, in due time,
yield her increase for our use and benefit.
　　　　—THE BOOK OF COMMON PRAYER

Clear moon,
Frost soon.
　　　　—OLD ENGLISH RHYME

Cloudy mornings turn to clear afternoons.
　　　　—ENGLISH PROVERB

If ducks and drakes their wings do flutter high,
Or tender colts upon their backs do lie;
If sheep do bleat or play and skip about,
Or swine hide by straw bearing on their snout;
If oxen lick themselves against the hair,
Or grazing kine to feed apace appear;
If cattle bellow, gazing from below,
Or if dogs' entrails rumble to and fro;
If doves and pigeons in the evening come
Later than usual to their dovehouse home;
If crows and daws do oft themselves bewet,
Or ants and pismires home apace do get;
If in the dust hens do their pinions shake,
Or by their flocking a great number make;
If swallows fly upon the water low,
Or woodlice seem in armies for to go;
If flies or gnats or fleas infest and bite,
Or sting more than their wont by day and night;
If toads hie home or frogs do croak amain,
Or peacocks cry—soon look for rain.

—ANONYMOUS

Oh, what a blamed uncertain thing
  This pesky weather is;
It blew and snew and then it thew,
  And now, by jing, it's friz.

—PHILANDER JOHNSON

One of the daintiest joys of spring is the falling of soft rain among blossoms. The shining and apparently weightless drops come pattering into the maytree with a sound of soft laughter; one alights on a white petal with a little inaudible tap; then petal and raindrop fall together down the steeps of green and white, accompanied by troops of other petals, each with her attendant drop and her passing breath of scent.   —MARY WEBB

> Pale moon doth rain,
>   Red moon doth blow,
> White moon doth neither
>   Rain nor snow.
>   —OLD ENGLISH RHYME

There is really no such thing as bad weather, only different kinds of good weather.   —JOHN RUSKIN

When Clouds appear like Rocks
   and Towers,
The Earth's refreshed by frequent
   Showers.

                    —JOHN CLARIDGE

When the clouds rise in terraces of white, soon will the country of the corn priests be pierced with arrows of rain.

—ZUNI INDIAN SAYING

Rain is good for vegetables, and for animals who eat those vegetables, and for the animals who eat those animals.

—SAMUEL JOHNSON

Sweet April showers Do bring May flowers.

—THOMAS TUSSER

Truly in the East
The white bean
And the great corn-plant
Are tied with the white lightning.
Listen! rain approaches!
The voice of the bluebird is heard.
Truly in the East
The white bean
And the great squash
Are tied with the rainbow.

—LOUVA DAHOZY

A fly on your nose;
You slap and it goes;
If it comes back again
It will bring a good rain.
—ENGLISH RHYME

And a thousand recollections
   Weave their bright hues into woof
As I listen to the patter
   Of the soft rain on the roof.
—COATES KINNEY

For as the rain cometh down and the snow from the heaven, and returneth not thither, but watereth the earth, and maketh it bring forth and bud, that it may give seed to the sower, and bread to the eater.   —ISAIAH

God sendeth down water from Heaven, and causeth the earth to revive after it hath been dead. Verily, herein is a sign of the resurrection unto people who hearken.
—XVI, THE KORAN

In the country they say, "We'll come when it rains." When the soft rains come soaking through the day and into the night, they go visiting, they sit around the kitchen table in a dry place and talk of children and crops.
—YVETTE NELSON

O rain! with your dull two-fold sound,
The clash hard by, and the murmur all round!
—Samuel Taylor Coleridge

Rain from the East;
Rain three days at least.
—American rhyme

The big rain comes dancing to the earth. —Lord Byron

A dry May and a leaking June
Make the farmer whistle a merry tune.
—Old English rhyme

If the first of July be rainy weather,
It will rain, more or less, for four weeks together.
—Old English rhyme

The thirsty earth soaks up the rain,
And drinks, and gapes for drink again.
The plants suck in the earth, and are
With constant drinking fresh and fair.
—Abraham Cowley

When the grass is dry at morning light
Look for the rain before the night.
—ENGLISH RHYME

Beautiful snow! It can do nothing wrong.

—J. W. WATSON

Deep snow in the Winter; tall grain in the Summer.
—ESTONIAN PROVERB

I love snow, and all forms
Of the radiant frost.
—PERCY BYSSHE SHELLEY

No cloud above, no earth below—
A universe of sky and snow.
—JOHN GREENLEAF WHITTIER

While we slept, these formal gardens
Worked into their disguise. The Warden's
Judas and tulip trees awake
In ermine. Here and there a flake
Of white falls from the painted scene,
Or a dark scowl of evergreen
Glares through the shroud, or a leaf dumps
Its load and the soft burden slumps
Earthward like a fainting girl.
—CECIL DAY LEWIS

TIME AND CYCLES

Sweet is the breath of morn, her rising
   sweet
With charm of earliest birds; pleasant
   the sun
When first on this delightful land he
   spreads
His orient beams on herb, tree, fruit,
   and flower.

—JOHN MILTON

❧ ❧ ❧

Flowers and even fruit are only the beginning. In the seed lies the life and the future.   —MARION ZIMMER BRADLEY

The Infinite has written its name on the heavens in shining stars, and on the earth in tender flowers.
                                                    —JEAN PAUL RICHTER

Still—in a way—nobody sees a flower—really—it is so small—we haven't time—and to see takes time, like to have a friend takes time.   —GEORGIA O'KEEFFE

I shall soon be laid in the quiet grave—thank God for the quiet grave—O! I can feel the cold earth upon me—the daisies growing over me—O for this quiet—it will be my first.   —JOHN KEATS

First the blade, then the ear, after that the full corn in the ear.   —MARK, 4:28

It is easy for me to link salvation and compost. Compost has an almost mystical quality. It is made up of anything that is or was alive and is biodegradable—straw, spoiled hay, grass clippings, animal remains, manure, garbage, flesh, table scraps, etc. A compost heap represents immortality. Nothing dies as such. All living things complete their cycle and return to the pool of life. There is neither beginning nor end, only the inexorable turning of the great wheel: growth, decay, death, and rebirth. —WILLIAM LONGGOOD

Nothing that is can pause or stay;
The moon will wax, the moon will
wane,
The mist and cloud will turn to rain,
The rain to mist and cloud again,
Tomorrow be today.
        —HENRY WADSWORTH LONGFELLOW

Morning is the best of all times in the garden. The sun is not yet hot. Sweet vapors rise from the earth. Night dew clings to the soil and makes plants glisten. Birds call to one another. Bees are already at work.
                    —WILLIAM LONGGOOD

Observe this dew-drenched rose of Tyrian gardens
A rose today. But you will ask in vain
Tomorrow what it is; and yesterday
It was the dust, the sunshine, and the rains.
—LUCRETIUS

One by one the flowers close,
Lily and dewy rose
Shutting their tender petals from the moon.
—CHRISTINA ROSSETTI

One of the recurring pleasures of planting bulbs in autumn is walking amongst them in spring and wondering
how on earth you did it. Bulb planting is torture. The
basket never seems to diminish and yet stamina in the
lower back does. Eventually there seems nothing to pull
you upright over and over again but a series of protesting
muscles. It's one of the most laborious and tiring jobs,
even so, lifting resistant clods of turf, carefully placing
each plum-sized golden bulb in the ground, you know
you are burying amongst the worms spoonfuls of colour:
crimson, rose, purple, or magenta; white flecked with
mauve, pink running into amethyst and white. And finally, after straightening your back and stamping back
the grass, leaving no evidence of your hours of labour,
you can think: why, there's only six months to wait before
being confounded.
—MIRABEL OSLER

Shed no tears! O shed no tears!
The flower will bloom another year.
Weep no more! O weep no more!
Young buds sleep in the root's white core.

—JOHN KEATS

Some men go into the wilderness to slay, and they come home bearing their burdens of fish and game. Others—the gentle hunters—go armed with basket and trowel, for the quarry they would track are green growing things that they hope to keep alive—ferns and flowers and the tender roots that will grow to lusty shrubs. . . . The gentle hunter has always his quarry beside him in his garden. In spring he awaits its awakening, watches its burgeoning in summer, sees its leaves turn and fall in the shortening days of autumn and in winter can rest content in the certainty that the cycle will start afresh when spring comes again.

—RICHARDSON WRIGHT

The stillness of the early morning scene enables me to take in and enjoy many things which pass me by during the bustle of the day. First there are the scents, which seem even more generous with their offerings than they are in the evening. The good old-fashioned dog-rose in the hedgerow was almost effusive in its fragrance and the leaves of the Sweetbriar or Eglantine, so loved by the Elizabethans, had a richness, which must have been caused by the dew, far surpassing anything they usually provide, except after rain.

—ROSEMARY VEREY

[In the garden] the door is always open into the "holy"—growth, birth, death. Every flower holds the whole mystery in its short cycle, and in the garden we are never far away from death, the fertilizing, good, *creative* death.

—MAY SARTON

When in these fresh mornings I go into my garden before anyone is awake, I go for the time being into perfect happiness. In this hour divinely fresh and still, the fair face of every flower salutes me with a silent joy that fills me with infinite content; each gives me its color, its grace, its perfume, and enriches me with the consummation of its beauty. All the cares, perplexities, and griefs of existence, all the burdens of life slip from my shoulders and leave me with the heart of a little child that asks nothing beyond its present moment of innocent bliss.   —CELIA THAXTER

Gather ye rose-buds while ye may:
Old time is still a-flying.

—ROBERT HERRICK

All gardens are the product of leisure. It is no good looking for gardens in a society which needs all its energies to survive.

—DEREK CLIFFORD

I hate to be reminded of the passage of time, and in a garden of flowers one can never escape from it. It is one of the charms of a garden of grass and evergreens, that there for a while one is allowed to hug the illusion that time tarries. —E. V. Lucas

If we persist, I do not doubt that by age 96 or so we will all have gardens we are pleased with, more or less.
—Henry Mitchell

It is apparent that no lifetime is long enough in which to explore the resources of a few square yards of ground.
—Alice M. Coats

There is nothing like the first hot days of spring when the gardener stops wondering if it's too soon to plant the dahlias and starts wondering if it's too late. Even the most beautiful weather will not allay the gardener's notion (well-founded, actually) that he is somehow too late, too soon, or that he has too much stuff going on or not enough.
—Henry Mitchell

These flowers, which were splendid and sprightly,
Waking in the dawn of the morning,
In the evening will be a pitiful frivolity,
Sleeping in the night's cold arms.
                    —PEDRO CALDERON DE LA BARCA

Train up a fig-tree in the way it should go, and when you
are old sit under the shade of it.   —CHARLES DICKENS

Yesterday I sat in a field of violets for a long time perfectly
still, until I really sank into it—into the rhythm of the
place, I mean—then when I got up to go home I couldn't
walk quickly or evenly because I was still in time with the
field.   —ANNE MORROW LINDBERGH

GOD IN THE GARDEN

To cultivate a Garden is to walk
with God.

—CHRISTIAN BOVEE

A garden is a lovesome thing, God wot!
Rose plot, fringed pool, ferned grot—
The veriest school
Of peace, and yet the fool
Contends that God is not—
Not God! In gardens when the eve is cool?
Nay, but I have a sign,
'Tis very sure God walks in mine.

—THOMAS EDWARD BROWN

God almighty first planted a garden. And, indeed, it is the purest of human pleasures. —FRANCIS BACON

Heaven is under our feet as well as over our heads.

—HENRY DAVID THOREAU

That God once loved a garden
We learn from Holy writ.
And seeing gardens in the spring
I well can credit it.

—WINIFRED MARY LETTS

He who sows the ground with care and diligence acquires a greater stock of religious merit than he could gain by the repetition of ten thousand prayers. —ZOROASTER

> The kiss of the sun for pardon,
>   The song of the birds for mirth;
> One is nearer God's Heart in the garden
>   Than anywhere else on earth.
>   —DOROTHY FRANCES GURNEY

> The little cares that fretted me,
>   I lost them yesterday . . .
> Among the husking of the corn
>   Where drowsy poppies nod
> Where ill thoughts die and good are born
>   Out in the fields with God.
>   —ANONYMOUS

The Lord God planted a garden eastward in Eden; and there he put the man whom he had formed. —GENESIS II

Flowers are the sweetest things God ever made and forgot to put a soul into.

                           —HENRY WARD BEECHER

Little flower—but if I could understand
What you are, root and all, and all in all,
I should know what God and man is.
                              —ALFRED, LORD TENNYSON

To create a little flower is the labour of ages.
                              —WILLIAM BLAKE

The best place to seek God is in a garden. You can dig for
Him there.   —GEORGE BERNARD SHAW

INDEX

ABOUT THE EDITOR

Maria Polushkin Robbins is the author of twelve cook-
books and several children's books. She has edited two
other quotation collections: *A Cook's Alphabet of Quotations* and *Puss in Books: A Collection of Great Cat
Quotations*, both from The Ecco Press. She lives with
her husband in East Hampton, New York.